The Sustainable(ish) Guide to Green Parenting

The Sustainable(ish) Guide to Green Parenting

Guilt-free eco-ideas for raising your kids

Jen Gale

GREEN TREE
LONDON • OXFORD • NEW YORK • NEW DELHI • SYDNEY

GREEN TREE
Bloomsbury Publishing Plc
50 Bedford Square, London, WC1B 3DP, UK
29 Earlsfort Terrace, Dublin 2, Ireland

BLOOMSBURY, GREEN TREE and the Green Tree logo are trademarks of
Bloomsbury Publishing Plc

First published in Great Britain 2021

A catalogue record for this book is available from the British Library

Library of Congress Cataloguing-in-Publication data has been applied for

ISBN: TPB: 978-1-4729-8457-9; eBook: 978-1-4729-8458-6;
ePDF: 978-1-4729-8459-3

2 4 6 8 10 9 7 5 3 1

Typeset in Minion by Deanta Global Publishing Services, Chennai, India
Printed and bound in Great Britain by CPI Group (UK) Ltd, Croydon CR0 4YY

The Forest Stewardship Council® (FSC®) is a global, not-for-profit organization
dedicated to the promotion of responsible forest management worldwide.
FSC defines standards based on agreed principles for responsible forest stewardship
that are supported by environmental, social, and economic stakeholders. To learn
more, visit www.fsc.org. By choosing this product, you are supporting
responsible management of the world's forests.

To find out more about our authors and books visit www.bloomsbury.com
and sign up for our newsletters

For parents everywhere – keep on keeping on.

Contents

Introduction

Having kids is a life-changing experience. It changes your life in all the obvious ways – less sleep, less disposable income, fewer nights out, a whole new set of challenges. More joy, more laughter, and more love than you ever knew was possible.

It's also one of the most climate-unfriendly things we can do as individuals. According to Mike Berners-Lee, in his brilliant book *How Bad are Bananas?* where he lists the carbon footprint of pretty much everything, having a child results in the release of anywhere between 210 and 5000+ tonnes of CO_2 depending on how you raise them, and whether they continue to live in an eco-friendly way once they've left home.

Now let's be clear here, the very last thing I want to do is to shame anyone, or to up your levels of guilt/anxiety. Having kids or not is a hugely personal decision. It's your decision to make (we have two kids, I'm not judging anyone) and if you're reading this book, the chances are that decision has already been made. However, what we can take from this is that we as parents can have a huge 'impact on the impact' that both we and our kids have on the planet.

With a whole new precious life to look after, comes a whole new perspective on the world, and maybe even our place in it. We see the future differently. We start to look beyond our own lifespans and look towards the kind of world our kids might be living in when they're all grown up. The expectation (certainly in more recent times) has been that each generation will be better off than the one before – that they will be more affluent, and that their quality of life will be better. We almost took it for granted.

And now we're suddenly faced with the stark reality that this new generation may be one of the first to be facing a significantly poorer future than we were able to look forward to as children.

We look to the future, to *their* future, only to be hit by the realisation that the 'someday' impact of our rapidly warming planet is now very much an impact that will be seen in the lifetime of our new child.

In 2018 the IPCC (Inter-governmental Panel on Climate Change) told us we had just 12 years to make 'unprecedented changes' if we were to limit climate change to 1.5°C above pre-industrial levels. We're currently on course for a 3–5 °C rise by 2100. And while I personally wouldn't be able to tell if my cuppa was at 97 °C or 95.5 °C, the planet can tell. At or below 1.5 °C, things will change, but in a way that we, and the planet's ecosystems, can adapt to. If nothing changes and we continue on the current trajectory, our kids are looking at a very different world, with rising sea levels causing a loss of land for living and growing food on. We are already seeing climate refugees – people having to move from their homes due to the encroachment of the sea, or because land that could once be farmed is now too dry, or it floods and destroys crops. Our kids are potentially looking at a more crowded planet, with less habitable land, less drinkable water, less available food, more severe weather events more frequently, more disputes and more exploitation of both people and planet.

If you've read *The Sustainable(ish) Living Guide*, you'll know that uplifting starts to books are not my forte, but I think we need to be clear about what the future could be. Not to scare the crap out of you and paralyse you with anxiety, but to show you what's at stake.

The future I've just described is not what any of us wants, but it's the future we're creating for our kids if nothing changes. If *we* don't change. Yes, we need governments to take radical action. Yes, we need businesses to make huge changes. But we also need to make change ourselves, and together we absolutely CAN make a difference.

In that IPCC report, they called for 'unprecedented change' and that sounds pretty daunting, doesn't it? But, actually, all it means is doing something we haven't done before. As a new parent (or indeed at any stage of parenting), everything we do is unprecedented! We're constantly learning new skills, doing new things. We've got 'unprecedented' nailed down. Now all we need to do is to take those skills of adaptation, learning and resilience and use them to make some better choices for the planet. Simple, right?!

Well … yes, kind of. Lots of the changes and ideas I'm sharing in this book are simple. There's no rocket science, no silver bullet, no secret blend of herbs and spices that I'm going to share. These really are simple changes, many of them akin to the kinds of things our grandparents were doing just a couple of generations ago. But just because things are simple doesn't mean they're easy.

We live in a society where we're told over and over again that more is better, that new is better. We're bombarded with literally thousands of messages a day telling us that our lives will be better, easier, if we buy x, y or z. That we'll be more beautiful, richer or more successful if we have the latest gadget or that shiny new pair of shoes. Our lives are busier than they have ever been. Convenience trumps all. More often than not we choose the quickest and easiest options, not because we don't care, but because we're busy, and tired, and stressed. We fall into very unintentional habits.

And when it boils down to it, a lot of what I'm going to share in this book is all about changing habits. Creating a new, sustainable(ish) normal. Making changes to lifelong habits is hard (but that doesn't mean we're not going to make a start…!). And when we're making changes in not only our own habits but doing it as a family, it's even harder (again, not an excuse not to start).

Your partner might not be on the same page as you.

Your kids might not be on the same page as you.

And there's a teeny chance well-meaning grandparents and relatives might not be on the same page as you.

If I lived alone, I reckon I'd be pretty hardcore – I like to think I'd happily go without crisps, I'd cycle a lot more for travel, I'd have less stuff. But I don't live alone. I live with a husband, two kids, and a dog. All of whom, frustratingly, have their own wants, needs and opinions (even, it would seem, the dog) and have frustratingly rejected my suggestion of a benign dictatorship where I'm allowed to have final say over all decisions. Which means the 'c-word' – compromise – has to come into play much of the time. We make slower progress, or sometimes even no progress, on many things. Some of the changes we've tried just haven't worked for the kids (using bar soap to wash their hands is one that springs to mind). So we've had to compromise to find a way that works for everyone, which might not be the 100 per cent 'green' choice but that is still a better choice, and one we can all live with.

Let's be very clear right from the start – I'm not a parenting expert. My kids will attest to that. I'm not going to tell you what to do, how to get your kids to sleep, what they should or shouldn't eat, how to get them to put their bloody shoes on in the morning as you attempt to make it to school on time, or how many hours of screen-time they should have. #sorrynotsorry

I'm also not an environmental scientist. We don't live off-grid. We're not self-sufficient in fruit and veg. We aren't #plasticfree or #zerowaste. We are **not** perfectly green.

What I am is a knackered mum of two, with a firm belief that we can make a difference. That our individual actions really do matter. That in amongst the overwhelm, and the busyness, and the never-ending anxiety and guilt of parenting we can make some simple switches to help the planet, by embracing the power of 'sustainable(ish)'.

My make do and mend year

My own journey into all things sustainable(ish) began with the slightly random decision that we should spend a year buying nothing new as a family. The kids were four and two at the time, so not really old enough to have much of a say in the matter, and I have often thought over the following years what a different experience it would be now, as my kids grow and become more aware of 'stuff'.

At the start of the year I already thought we were pretty green because, after all, we were pretty diligently separating our recycling. But I had never really stopped and thought about what we were buying and the impact that it might be having on the planet, never mind joined the dots between what we were buying and what we were throwing away. But during that year I was forced to confront lots of issues that I think previously I had somehow been choosing to look away from – things like fast fashion and resource depletion, and indeed climate change (it had yet to be re-named the climate crisis/emergency). I hadn't really realised just how much of our consumption was unconscious, with no real thought given to what we were buying, or where we were getting it from, other than where we might be able to find it cheapest. The enforced stop gap between making the decision 'we need this' (or even 'we want this') and sourcing it secondhand gave me the breathing space to make a much more deliberate decision about whether in fact we really did need that item, or whether we could actually make do with something else we already had.

I learned lots of practical skills during the year, like patching the many, many pairs of jeans that we all seemed to go through the knees of, and even fulfilled a 'make do and mend' stereotype by darning the odd pair of socks.

But the biggest lesson learned, my takeaway from the year, was that **as 'just one person', or even 'just one family' we really can make a difference**. In the years that have passed since then, as awareness of the climate crisis has grown and calls for action have become increasingly urgent, there's a lot of debate over who should be responsible for taking action – the government, businesses or individuals. And the answer clearly is all three. We need *everyone* to be taking action on this issue – it's so big, so overwhelming, so urgent, that we won't achieve anywhere near the scale of change that we need without everyone on board. I know that there are people who refer to individual actions like giving up disposable coffee cups as 'tinkering around the edges', or even 'wafting at a house fire with a tea towel', and who call for a whole new economic and political system. And that might very well be what we need. But as the aforementioned ordinary knackered working mum of two, I don't know how to overthrow the government, and even if I did, I've got to make sure I'm back in time for the school run, so quite honestly I'm not sure it's something I can commit to. But as that ordinary knackered mum I have tremendous power over our family's buying decisions, and through that power I can put pressure on businesses to be more sustainable. And as my confidence in my ability to effect change grows, I can also make my voice heard with my local MP, and maybe start to engage with businesses on social media, and create ripples of change that spread out through my family and friends.

You don't need to spend a year buying nothing new to come to these realisations (I've done that bit for you), but please don't ever doubt that as just one person, as a knackered, overwhelmed, time-poor parent, you can make a difference and help to create a healthier future for our children.

The 'ish' is the important bit. What works for you won't be the same as what works for another family. And that's OK. What works for you now might not be what works in a few months' or years' time. And that's OK. We are unique. Our families are unique. We each have our own set of circumstances and challenges that means that our 'easy' might be someone else's 'hard', or vice versa. Be gentle with yourselves. Sometimes (in life as well as in sustainable(ish) stuff) it might feel like it's two steps forwards and one back. But it's all progress. It's all learning, and adapting and figuring it out. And *no-one* has it all figured out (life, parenting, or the eco stuff…).

I talk about sustainable**(ish)**, plastic-free**(ish)**, zero waste**(ish)**, because I think without the 'ish' those terms are pretty daunting. There aren't many (any?) people who can be perfectly plastic-free, or zero-waste, especially not with kids in tow, but we can all be plastic-free(ish) – we can make different choices to REDUCE the amount of single-use plastic we use, whether that's an entirely plastic-free option, or one that means we use less plastic, less often. It feels way more do-able that way, and I think we're much more likely to make a start, and to have a go, if we know that we're not expected to be perfect.

Remember that this is a marathon and not a sprint. And that no-one's expecting you to run that marathon tomorrow from a chocolate encrusted, sofa-bound start. We're looking to make changes that we can stick to, that will last the distance, rather than an over-ambitious New Year's fitness regime that starts off with Tigger-like enthusiasm and daily workouts, and ends nine days later with Eeyore levels of motivation and self-esteem.

Bringing a new life into the world brings with it a tsunami of (unprecedented) change, at a time when we have very little headspace, time or energy for doing research. And at a time when we might well be feeling anxious about the choices we're making for a whole variety of reasons. The very last thing I want to do is to pile on more pressure, more anxiety or more guilt.

This book is for you if…

- You've never really thought a huge amount about the state of the planet, but it's suddenly hit you that there might be some 'not so good stuff' going on…

- You're feeling like you want to 'do your bit' for your kids, and for the planet, but you're already pretty snowed under with general life stuff and feel anxious at the thought of adding yet more stuff to your to-do list…
- You were pretty green pre-kids, but you found that for a while the demands of keeping a small person alive and entertained took centre stage (rightly and understandably so) and you want to work out how to get back on track, and how to adapt your green habits now you've got a baby in tow…
- You've got older kids who are coming to you with questions from school, or wanting to get involved with the youth climate movement, and you feel like you want to support them but you're not really sure what you can do or how to do it…

What I hope I can do with this book, is to show you some options. To make it easy (or, at the very least, easier) to find out the information you want, and then to make informed choices about what might work for you and your family.

Before we start

As a parent you already have a 'to do' list as long as your arm. You are probably bombarded with well-meaning advice and a scroll of your Facebook feed will tell you five different ways to do the same thing, and that each one is absolutely THE RIGHT one to do. You will feel guilty for the things you do, and guilty for the things you don't do.

There is a huge amount of overwhelm that comes with parenting, especially in the early days. And there's a huge amount of overwhelm that comes with thinking about the climate crisis and what the hell we might be able to do about it.

With overwhelm, comes paralysis. It's like me venturing into John Lewis to replace our ancient and very tatty towels and seeing so many different choices for towels – ultra soft cotton, Egyptian cotton, plush supima cotton (nope, no idea either), silky suvin cotton (again, no idea); face cloth, hand towel, bath towel, bath sheet … and that's before we even look at colours and patterns. What should have been a simple purchase ends up in a massive amount of overwhelm and no towels bought (or maybe this is just me…).

The best antidote for overwhelm and anxiety is action. Just buy a bloody towel. It doesn't have to be THE towel to end all towels. It just has to do the job.

So take action. Imperfect action. Read and DO.

The smallest step is still a step, and that small step gives you the momentum and motivation for the next one.

5 TOP TIPS FOR GETTING STARTED

1 THINK ABOUT YOUR WHY

My why, when it boils down to it, is my kids. Our kids. All of our kids, and their futures. When it all feels a bit much, when I'm tempted to just jack it all in, when I see other people carrying on as normal and there's part of me that wishes I didn't know what I know and that I too could do all that stuff with a clear conscience, it really helps to tune back into my why. It doesn't always make it easier, but it reminds me why it's important.

2 FOCUS ON WHAT WORKS FOR YOU

What works for other people might not work for you. It doesn't matter. 'You do you babe' is an internet phrase that might make you want to vomit, but annoyingly it's actually a pretty good sentiment. Don't worry about what other people are doing – if they're 'ace-ing it' with reusable nappies that they made themselves from old t-shirts, and are weaning their baby on an entirely homegrown vegan diet – if that works for them, wish them well. If they're jetting off on multiple holidays a year and purchasing a holiday wardrobe for the kids each time, which they then just throw away (yes, I have heard of this happening) because it's 'too cheap to bother washing', don't waste your energy getting angry at them (maybe also don't wish them well though…) if you can't do anything to change that.

3 EMBRACE THE 'ISH'

As a society, it feels increasingly like we're polarising – we're left or right, leave or remain, vegan or not, drinkers or teetotal. We've lost sight of the middle ground. And, just as in life there's very little that is black and white, in all things eco there's very rarely a 'green and white'. There isn't this green hierarchy, where we start at the bottom as the very palest of greens, and move upwards in a linear fashion to the pinnacle of the greenest of all greens. What there is, is a myriad shades of green – and we'll be different shades of green in different areas of our lives, on different days of the week, and depending on how irritating the kids are being.

4 GO FOR THE EASY WINS

Especially at the start. Think about the changes that will be the least stressful, easiest to get everyone on board with, cheapest, and do those. It doesn't have to be hard to be worthwhile.

5 PICK ONE THING

Start off by picking one area to work on: maybe that's food, or clothes, or single-use plastic. And then pick ONE thing to change within that. So maybe that's eating less meat, buying fewer new clothes, or cutting down on single-use plastic in the bathroom. Then, again, pick ONE change within that – maybe that's one meat-free meal a week, or sorting through your wardrobe, or finding a plastic-free(ish) shampoo that works for you. Change happens ONE step at a time.

A note about how to use this book

More than anything, I want this book to help you to take action. Yes, I want you to buy it. I want you to read it, and enjoy it. But more than that, I want it to help you create planet-positive change.

The chapters are set out in rough age ranges, in a chronological order, starting with 'pre-baby', up to 'teens'. There will inevitably be some overlap – I've put holidays in the primary school section, but clearly you're probably (hopefully) going to be going on holiday before that point too. So work with it however works best for you – dip into the age groups that are relevant and use the index to look for the other bits you want. Or read it cover to cover, whatever works for you.

But each time you read, go and DO. (Unless you've got a newborn. In which case, read and then sleep if your baby is still asleep.)

There's room at the end of each chapter to create your action plan. This isn't intended to stress you out, and create more anxiety and guilt. It's there if you want it, to help to identify the changes you want to make, help you make them happen, and help you to give yourself a bloody big pat on the back when you tick them off.

Some basic principles

I've already given you the spoiler alert that there is no magic bullet when it comes to all things sustainable(ish), but there are some key principles that are useful to keep in mind, and that I'll refer back to throughout the book. If you read my previous book, *The Sustainable(ish) Living Guide*, some of these will be familiar to you, but a spot of revision never hurt anyone. And there's also some key statistics I want to share to ~~scare the pants off you~~ motivate you.

> ## DID YOU KNOW?
>
> A 2015 study into the environmental impact of household consumption published in the *Journal of Industrial Ecology* found that more than 60 per cent of global greenhouse gas emissions are a result of household consumption.

This statistic still blows my mind, and really illustrates the power that we have as consumers to act on the climate crisis. This quote by Emma Watson, actor and activist, sums it up pretty well:

'As consumers, we have so much power to change the world just by being careful in what we buy.'

One of the main things we can do, as individuals and as families, is to consume less. And in a society where the message we constantly hear is buy, buy, buy, this is a pretty counter-cultural, possibly even slightly revolutionary thing to do.

The pressure we live under to continuously consume is immense, and much of it is subliminal – so subtle we don't even really hear it, we just unwittingly take it in. When it comes to our kids, it ramps up a notch. One of the ways that we have come to show our love is to buy things. It can feel like there's this unspoken rule, that if you really love your precious new baby and your kids as they grow, you must buy All The Things, and you must buy them new. Right from the point of conception (and indeed even before, with ovulation kits, pregnancy tests, pre-pregnancy vitamins…) we're bombarded with information and adverts for all the 'must have' equipment that will make parenting a breeze, and give our little darlings every chance to unleash their inner protégé (even at three months old – *Baby Einstein* anyone?!). And this just gets worse as the kids grow up, with an additional side serving of peer pressure thrown in for good measure.

It's SO hard to resist. There will undoubtedly be some things that you want to buy new for your baby, or for your kids as they grow up, but how about we make a pledge right now for 'brand new' not to be the default option? To try and make slower, more thoughtful choices about the things we buy for them. To buy whilst thinking about not only the best thing for our kids, and the things that they/we want right now, but the best thing for our kids' futures, and for the life we want them to have as adults. In Native American culture, they have the concept of seven generation stewardship:

'In our every deliberation, we must consider the impact of our decisions on the next seven generations.'
                    Great Law of the Iroquois

Now I get that that sounds pretty worthy, and not a little bit exhausting, but it really doesn't have to be hard. And remember, no-one's expecting the 'best' choices, all the time. Just better choices, more of the time.

The buyerarchy of needs from the wonderfully talented artist Sarah Lazarovic is one of my very favourite things, and is something I am constantly urging people to print out and stick to their fridges, or to get

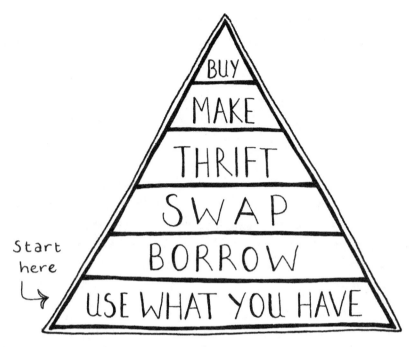

The buyerarchy of needs by Sarah Lazarovic

a mini copy and glue it to your purse or wallet. I've also said before that if I were ever brave enough to get a tattoo (I'm not), then this would be a definite contender.

Our knee-jerk response when we have a new baby/start a new hobby/get a new job/something breaks, is to rush out and buy everything we might need, and to buy them new. It's quick, it's convenient and we can have what we need with minimum effort, possibly without even leaving the sofa. But actually, with a little bit of thought, we may well be able to find the things we need without buying them new. Saving us some money, saving some of the planet's precious and finite resources, AND saving something that might otherwise have been thrown away to landfill. (Disclaimer: you may have to leave the sofa though, even if only to rummage through the drawer of doom to double-check for the batteries you think are probably in there to fix the baby monitor.)

The idea is that you start at the bottom of the triangle (use what you have) and work your way up – so that buying new is your last resort. So let's do just that…

USE WHAT YOU HAVE

One of the key 'pillars' of sustainable(ish) living and parenting, is '**the most sustainable version of anything is the one you already have**'.

In other words, we don't need to rush out and buy new 'green-er' versions of the things we already have. Yes, it's dull. It's got none of the excitement and far less potential for virtue signalling to your friends on Instagram, but them's the facts. And when it comes to kids, it's no different.

As I said, the most sustainable version of anything is the thing you already own. However, I do concede that if this is your first baby, it's unlikely that you'll already have a pram and everything else you need hanging around. But there will be some things that you already have that can be commandeered into a different role as you embark on your new life as a parent.

- Have you already got trousers with an elasticated waist? (If you haven't, I'm not sure we can be friends). Yes? Wear them rather than rush out to buy expensive maternity trousers.
- Do you already have a backpack? Yes? Use this for a changing bag!

BORROW

If you've timed it right and have friends who've already done their procreating, or have slightly older kids than yours, you could easily borrow the vast majority of what you need, from the Moses basket to the baby monitor, to the clothes. I've found that most people are desperate to have a clear-out – so you're doing them a favour too! Even if you haven't got friends or family with older kids, you'll be pleased to learn that there are a variety of increasingly accessible ways to borrow the things you need for the time you need them, and then to return them for someone else to use. I'll discuss options relevant to 'life stages' throughout the book, so keep your eyes peeled and bear this one in mind!

SWAP

You can swap all kinds of things informally with friends – toys, kids' books, maternity wear, clothes (children's and adults'), giving you an excuse for a get-together, and de/re-cluttering your house for free!

'Swishes' (clothes swaps) or 'Give and Take' events are larger, more organised events that you might find happening locally (some councils organise regular Give and Take Days – check your local council website).

THRIFT

Given that we once spent a year buying nothing new, it should come as no surprise that finding what we need secondhand is one of my very favourite things to do. Our year of not buying new transformed me from someone who used to have a desultory look around charity shops and leave empty-handed, to being one of those annoying people who answers, 'Oh this? I got it from the charity shop for £1.50,' when asked where I got something from. For someone who finds shopping with kids in tow akin to some kind of torture, I actually find charity shop shopping relatively un-stressful. Most have a toy corner where the kids are quite happy to scamper off to (or the buggy can be parked – #badmummy) while you dash round the rest of the shop keeping your fingers crossed that the charity shop fairies will have heard your wish for size 12 black jeans, or size 2 wellies.

All kinds of kids' things can be found secondhand for a fraction of their new price. Charity shops are the obvious one, but don't forget car boot sales (if you need to distract young ones while you have a good rummage, give each of the kids £1 and let them go K-RAZY!) – great for cheap toys, and also bundles of clothes. For babies and toddlers, NCT 'nearly new' sales can also be a godsend, with lots of bargains and hardly used stuff waiting to be snapped up. Do go prepared though – the ones I have been to have resembled a rugby scrum, and you need to have your best pointy elbows out if you want to bag the best stuff (not that I advocate pointy elbows near heavily pregnant women. Or indeed ever. Please don't write and complain).

Not all secondhand shopping has to be in-person – don't forget good old eBay, as well as sites like Preloved and Craigslist. They're especially useful if you're looking for specific brands or sizes, and if you don't have the time or patience to trawl the charity shops.

Secondhand stuff for free!

Sometimes you can find the things you want or need without even having to part with any of your hard-earned cash – especially the stuff that is only used for a short amount of time.

- ● ASKING FRIENDS AND FAMILY

  This almost goes without saying, but I'm still going to say it because I think a lot of the time we forget. At my kids' school for sports day they have to wear coloured t-shirts according to the house they're in. My kids needed yellow t-shirts and I was loath to buy one for it to be used for only a couple of hours. I put out a plea on my personal Facebook page and had two yellow t-shirts within the day!

- ● FREEGLE (WWW.ILOVEFREEGLE.ORG) AND FREECYCLE (WWW.UK.FREECYCLE.ORG)

  If you haven't heard of either of these, you need them in your life. It's such a simple concept – they hook up people with stuff they no longer need or want, with people who are looking for things. You simply find your local group on the website and sign up (for free). You can then browse the OFFERED items, and post your own WANTEDs. It's great for getting rid of stuff that the charity shops might not take, but still keeping them in use and out of landfill, and can be a great way to get things like first bikes or craft stuff for free. One person's trash and all that…

- ● OLIO (WWW.OLIOEX.COM)

  The Olio app originally started life to help redistribute food that would otherwise go to waste to those who could make use of it, but has now expanded so that users can add other things to it as well. Simply download the app (for free) and start exploring.

- ● BUY NOTHING GROUPS (WWW.BUYNOTHINGPROJECT. ORG)

  The Buy Nothing Project began in the USA as a 'hyper-local gifting economy' in 2013 and now has over 1 million participants in

25 countries around the world. At the time of writing there are around 70 groups in the UK, which run via Facebook and help to keep resources in use within local communities.

● LOCAL FACEBOOK GROUPS

There are a multitude of local Facebook selling groups, some of which also share items for free, or facilitate swaps – have a look to see what's near you.

Things you shouldn't buy secondhand

Whilst you can easily source at least 90 per cent of the things you want or need for your kids (or for that matter yourself), there are a few things that should always be bought brand new, due to safety concerns.

● MATTRESSES FOR MOSES BASKETS AND COTS

The Lullaby Trust is a charity that works to raise awareness of Sudden Infant Death Syndrome (SIDS – previously referred to as cot death) and recommends buying a new mattress for each child. Their website says:

'There is some research that found an increased chance of SIDS when using a secondhand mattress brought in from outside of the family home, although the link is not yet proven. To help reduce this risk, if you are using a secondhand mattress make sure the mattress you choose was previously completely protected by a waterproof cover, with no rips or tears and is in good condition. The mattress should also still be firm and flat to keep your baby sleeping safely.

Personally we didn't want to take the risk, and bought new Moses basket mattresses for both of ours, although we happily used the Moses basket that was donated to us from friends.

● CAR SEATS

The Royal Society for the Prevention of Accidents advises against using or buying secondhand car seats:

'You cannot be certain of its history. It may have been involved in an accident and the damage may not be visible. Very often instructions are missing from secondhand seats, which makes it more difficult to be sure that you are fitting and using it correctly. Secondhand seats are also likely to be older, to have suffered more wear and tear and may not be designed to current safety standards. If you must use a secondhand seat, only accept one from a family member or friend (don't buy one from a secondhand shop, through classified ads or online). Only accept one from a family member or friend if you are absolutely certain that you know its history, it comes with the original instructions and it is not too old.'

We bought new car seats for our eldest but then happily used them for his younger brother.

● BIKE HELMETS

The same thing applies to bike helmets as it does to car seats. They can be damaged internally with no external signs, meaning that they won't provide sufficient levels of protection in the case of an accident.

MAKE

If you're reading this with a young baby, or toddlers rampaging around the house, you may well be spitting your tea out right now at the idea that anyone has any time to make stuff. It might not seem like it right now, but the time WILL come when you are not only able to poo in peace, and drink a still-hot cuppa, but that you might even have the time/headspace/desire to make some things from scratch.

I've been known to drag out the sewing machine to make some simple stuff for the kids (only bunting and beanbags, don't worry, nothing too ambitious) and we've even got friends who made a bed for one of their kids (#showingoff).

When you make things yourself, you're neatly side-stepping the possibility that the things you're buying/using have been made by workers who are being treated unfairly and not being paid a living wage. And I guarantee that if you've spent a weekend slaving over constructing a bed for one of your little darlings, you're not going to simply chuck it out when you move house.

BUY

At the very top of the hierarchy is buying new.

No-one's saying never buy anything new again (although you certainly could – our year doing just that showed me that it is indeed more possible than we might imagine), but let's try and shift our buying behaviour so that instead of hitting Amazon for our instant fix of consumerism each time we need anything, we explore the other options first. And when we do buy new, let's try and give a little thought to who we want to give our hard-earned pennies to.

This quote is another contender for the tattoo I will never be cool enough to have:

> 'Every time we spend money, we're casting a vote for the kind of world we want.'
>
> Anna Lappé, author and sustainable food advocate

If we want a world ruled by a few gigantic tax-avoiding corporations, then by all means, please do continue to give your money to them. I agree with you, it is totally the most convenient (and often the cheapest) option. But we need to be careful what we wish for and remember that all of this convenience and the low cost comes at a price that is more than just the financial. It comes at the expense of workers, at the expense of the planet, and at the expense of our local high streets and independent retailers. Think about the kind of world you want, right now, and for your kids to grow up in. Do you want them to have a bustling high street? Do you want there to be local artisan markets, fairtrade goods, locally produced food? If you do, then remember that convenience doesn't have to be king. We have a choice.

The waste hierarchy

I never thought I would be a hierarchy geek, but given that this is the second one in just a few pages I may have to re-evaluate that. I also never used to give much (any) consideration to the things that we threw away. I chucked stuff in the bin, the bin lorry collected it, end of story. I had thrown my stuff 'away' without giving any thought to where this mythical land of 'away' might be, and any impact it might be having on the planet.

Yes, I think we all know that our rubbish goes to landfill. Or maybe we're even aware that our council burns our rubbish to create energy (so called energy from waste). But with an ever growing, ever more disposable society, the amount of waste we create is rapidly overwhelming the capacity of the planet to deal with it.

Not only are we rapidly running out of landfill space, the stuff that ends up there doesn't really break down in the way we think (if indeed we ever actually think about it at all). Because of the way that landfill sites work, its contents kind of ferment, rather than rot. They don't just magically dissolve into harmless substances – in fact, in the BBC's *The Secret Life of Landfill* documentary they unearthed an entirely readable newspaper (something that we all assume degrades pretty rapidly) from a site that was sealed in the 1980s. And when landfill rots, it produces methane, a greenhouse gas that is approximately 30 times more potent than carbon dioxide.

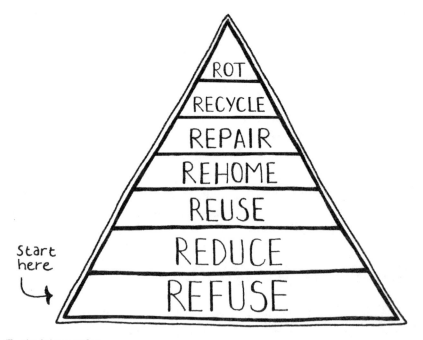

Waste hierarchy

There is no 'away'. All of our stuff – our clothes, our gadgets, the food we don't eat – has to go somewhere, and when it does, it's contributing to the climate crisis. And that's before we take into account the wasted materials and resources, and the carbon and water footprints of making the things in the first place.

So all of this is to say, one of the most powerful things we can do to help the planet is to throw less stuff away, which is where the wonderful waste hierarchy comes in.

Again, as with the buyerarchy of needs, the idea is that you start at the bottom with 'Refuse' and work your way up the hierarchy, with 'Rot' (landfill) being the final resort.

REFUSE

This might seem hard, especially when it comes to our kids. Few of us want to refuse them the things they want. But there are also a lot of things that we're told that they need, especially when they're new babies, that we could pretty easily refuse (*see* page 52).

REDUCE

Do you really need the 27 babygros that seem to have found their way into the chest of drawers? Do the kids really need quite so many toys? This isn't to say we have to live in pared-down minimalist homes (ours is very much not!), but let's try to be realistic about how many clothes one baby or child will actually wear.

REUSE

Keep reuse in mind when you're buying things – buying a reusable version of anything (water bottle, coffee, baby wipes, nappies…) is always going to better (environmentally speaking) than a single-use version. With the massive proviso that you do actually reuse them. According to environmental charity Hubbub, 69 per cent of us own a reusable cup, yet only 1 in 6 of us remembers to take it with us each time we get a takeaway drink. Reusable versions use up a whole heap more resources (and carbon) in their manufacture, so need to ***actually be reused*** in order for them to be more eco-friendly than their single-use counterparts.

REHOME

When we think of rehoming, most of us think about dropping off overflowing bin bags at the charity shop after a clear-out. We dump and run with a clear conscience that we've avoided landfill and helped a charity to raise some much-needed funds. But as I discussed in *The Sustainable(ish) Living Guide*, this isn't always the case – only 10–30 per cent of the clothes received by charity shops are actually sold on in the UK. The rest goes overseas to developing nations, or is sent to landfill if it's too far gone. I can only imagine that there is a similar scenario with kids' toys and books. Charity shop staff simply don't have the time and resources to fix and clean all the donations they receive. Anything that's broken or filthy will probably just be sent to landfill, meaning that all we've done is to pass on the problem to a middle man before it hits the tip. I'm not in any way suggesting that you don't donate your good quality items to your local charity shop, but please do ensure that they are just that – good quality. If you wouldn't buy it for your child, chances are no-one else will.

Remember that you can also offer items to friends and family, to your local Freecycle group, or sell them on eBay, at a car boot or a 'nearly new' sale.

REPAIR

Again, if you're reading this with a babe in arms or a toddler underfoot, you may well laugh slightly hysterically at the idea that anyone has the time to fix broken things, but again, I promise you this won't always be the case.

At the start of our year buying nothing new, I had never even sewn on a button, but by the end I was a whizz at imperfect yet functional mends. YouTube is your friend, as is #visiblemending (check it out on Instagram). And if all that feels a bit much, check out the Repair Café website (www.repaircafe.org) to see if you have a local event near you – these are pop-up 'cafes' that have volunteer fixers on hand to help you mend your broken stuff.

RECYCLE

The most important thing to note here, is that 'recycle' is almost at the very top of the hierarchy. It's one of the **last resorts**. Many of us will think that doing our recycling makes us official green heroes, but sadly that's not quite the case. Recycling is a complicated old business, and sometimes, despite our diligent adherence to the very particular (and very different from county to county) set of recycling guidelines laid out by the council and our very best efforts, our recycling might not even be recycled.

As we discovered in 2017 when China placed a ban on imports for plastic recycling, sometimes out of sight is out of mind, and unfortunately sometimes we can't guarantee that our recycling is actually recycled. Also bear in mind that recycling itself is not an innocuous process – it still uses energy (carbon) and in a lot of cases materials are 'downcycled' into lower quality products. That's not to say don't continue to separate and sort your recycling; please please do. And please check out the brilliant Recycle Now website (www.recyclenow.com) to find out what can be recycled near you, both kerbside and at the recycling centre. But just bear in mind that there are loads of layers of the hierarchy to explore before resorting to recycling.

ROT

If you've done all (or even some) of the above, you hopefully won't have a huge amount still left to go in your black bin. Doing a 'bin audit' can be a useful (if not hugely appealing) thing to do. Either pop on your (reusable) rubber gloves, and have a poke around in your black bin to get a rough idea of what's in there, or keep a piece of paper by the kitchen bin and make a note each time you put something in over the course of a week. Whichever way you choose, the idea is that you gather some info about exactly what you're throwing away. There's a teeny chance that even if you're super anal about putting the right stuff in the right recycling boxes, other members of your family aren't quite so thorough…

We took part in a 'rubbish diet' a few years ago and found that simply by recycling our 'stretchy plastic' (fruit and veg bags etc.) with the carrier bag recycling (this is legit, I checked!) and finding a way to home compost our food waste, we reduced our black bin's contents by at least two thirds.

Options for composting food waste

Food waste is a HUGE issue when it comes to the climate crisis.

- A land mass the size of Canada and India combined is used to grow food that is never eaten.
- If food waste were a country, it would be the third largest emitter of greenhouse gases, after the USA and China.
- Fifty per cent of food waste occurs in the home.

All of these statistics are shocking, but it's the last one that really blows my mind, and also empowers me hugely. It shows how we really can create large-scale change by tweaking some things at home.

Having kids definitely ramps up the food waste, with discarded crusts, apples with one bite taken out of (why????!!), and the meals you've lovingly slaved over that are then rejected despite having been eaten happily just the previous week (*! < **&@). I'll share some ideas for reducing food waste later on (*see* page 119), but for now let's have a quick look at ways we can keep our food waste out of landfill (where it ferments and emits methane).

Council kerbside food recycling

If you have one of these, use it! Check what you can put in there, and then make it happen. You might need to do a little light training for the other members of your household!

Regular compost heap

If you have a compost heap, you can use it for all your uncooked food waste, so things like fruit and veg peelings, tea bags, coffee grounds (although these are also very good as plant fertiliser) etc. You mustn't put cooked food or meat in there though.

Hot composter

We have one of these called a Green Johanna (www.greatgreensystems.com) and many councils subsidise them for their residents if they don't offer a food waste collection service. I have no idea how it works (I can only assume some kind of actual magic) but we can put in not only our garden waste, but also our food waste including cooked food and meat. It's been an absolute godsend for us, hugely reducing the contents of our black bin. (And we've had no trouble with rats, just in case you were wondering.) Once it's worked its magic, you extract what's at the bottom and dig it into your garden. Be warned – it won't be nice, crumbly, innocuous compost like you buy in bags (or at least ours isn't). It's a bit stinky, so you want to have somewhere to dig it into, rather than using it as compost for potted plants etc.

Bokashi bin

With these, you put your food waste (including meat and cooked food) into smallish bins, and add a special bran thing (again, magic) and it kind of pickles the food waste. The fermentation process takes about 2–3 weeks and then the resultant food waste pickle can then be added to a regular compost heap, or dug into flower beds etc.

Wormery

These can be a really fun project to do with the kids, and have the advantage that if you've not got access to outdoor space, then you can have a mini one indoors. I'm reliably informed by 'wormologist' Anna at The Urban Worm (www.urbanworm.co.uk) that they don't smell!

Share Waste (www.sharewaste.com)

Share Waste is a platform that connects people who want to recycle their kitchen scraps with people who already have compost heaps or wormeries. There's an interactive map to search for people accepting waste near you – definitely worth a look!

A quick(ish) word on plastic

Tackling plastic use is often one of the first changes that many people want to make when it comes to the planet. And understandably so – once we start to notice it, we realise just how ubiquitous it is. I think one of the reasons that it has caught our collective imaginations so much is that it's very easy to see the cause and effect. We drink from a plastic water bottle, and then see plastic bottles littering our streets, or some of the heart-rending pictures of ocean and beach pollution as we scroll through social media. When we unpack the supermarket shop we're left with a whole bag full of plastic packaging that more often than not we have no option other than to add it to our landfill bin. And it can feel really overwhelming, especially when you've got kids, no time, and very little headspace, and they want all the snacks, all the time.

If it helps you to feel even a little less guilt-ridden and anxious each time you unpack your online shop, let me tell you that I think plastic packaging from food is one of THE hardest things to tackle. For ages and ages, I avoided it – it was very firmly in my 'too hard' box. And even though I'm now having a go, we are very, very far from plastic-free in the kitchen (and indeed the rest of the house). That's not to say we can't do anything, and that there aren't some really quick and easy swaps to make, but hopefully to reassure that if you still feel like you're sending a small plastic mountain to landfill each week, you're not 'failing'. As with anything, it's about embracing the 'ish' and finding out what works for you and your family.

Remember also that (whispers) not all plastic is bad plastic. (I'm whispering for fear of being pilloried by the hardcore zero waste-ers…). Lots of plastic is very useful – Lego has been an absolute live-saver in our house. As have plastic encased iPads, Tupperware and all manner of plastic toys (what did kids even play with before plastic…?). It's also clearly revolutionised healthcare, and in the right place is a hugely useful substance.

It's *single-use* plastic that we really want to focus on. Plastic is so useful because it's robust, durable and incredibly long lasting – all qualities that mean when we use it for single-use stuff, it hangs around for a long, long time afterwards, with the potential to end up in the environment and our waterways.

THE 'BIG FOUR' MOST COMMONLY USED SINGLE-USE PLASTICS:

1 Carrier bags
The introduction of the 5p levy on single-use carrier bags here in the UK saw a dramatic drop in the amount being used, but also an unforeseen consequence of an increase in the number of so-called 'bags for life' being used, which confusingly may have actually increased the total volume of plastic used (given that bags for life are much thicker).

I'd like to think that we've all got pretty used to taking our bags with us now when we do the supermarket shop, and there is the option to tick 'no bags' on most online shops (although whether they actually take any notice of said tick is another matter).

For added sustainable(ish) points, pop some reusable produce bags in with your bigger bags when you do your shop, and use these for loose fruit and veg.

2 Water bottles

According to Refill (www.refill.org.uk) one million bottles are bought around the world every single minute, and that figure is projected to go up by 20 per cent by 2021, and we use seven billion plastic bottles each year in the UK. Clearly, carrying your own refillable water bottle is key, and remembering to take it with you each time you go out so that your kids don't spend 20 minutes of what should have been a 10-minute trip into town complaining that they're 'dying of thirst' and you have to buy them a bottle of water (not that I'm speaking from bitter experience here or anything). Yes, I know it feels like yet another thing to add to the weight of the already bulging changing bag/rucksack, but the planet will thank you for it. You can get collapsible bottles that concertina down when empty, which helps a little bit. And once we're in the habit of remembering baby bottles or snacks when they're tiny, it's a small step to translate that into remembering water bottles as they get bigger.

Top tip: Download the Refill app to your phone to find places where you can refill your bottles when you're out and about. Also, don't be afraid just to ask in cafes etc.

3 Coffee cups

Collectively in the UK we use 7.5 million disposable coffee cups a day, and because they're a mix of cardboard and plastic (the lining that stops the coffee seeping out into your lap) they're difficult to recycle. A decent reusable coffee cup that keeps your cuppa hot and doesn't spill can feel like the Holy Grail. My favourite is the Kleen Kanteen – it keeps hot drinks hot for up to 12 hours, is non-spill so I can just chuck it in my bag, and has a lid I can drink out of whilst on the move.

4 Straws

Apparently, Americans use enough straws each day to circle the planet 2.5 times! And while most able-bodied adults are more than capable of managing without one, there's no denying that kids do love a straw. The ban on plastic straws, stirrers and ear buds that came into effect in England in October 2020 will hopefully have a similar effect to the plastic bag change, but remember that single-use paper straws are still a single-use item and in an ideal world we simply wouldn't bother. If your kids aren't really that fussed about straws, try to remember to say 'no straw please' if you're braving a family meal out in a restaurant or cafe. If they're partial to a straw and it adds to the excitement of the occasion, you get all the brownie points for taking your own reusable straw with you.

Confession: We have a set of reusable straws (possibly actually two) but I very rarely remember to take them out with us. And even if I do, I am then very unlikely to remember to say 'No straw please', thus rendering said reusables unusable.

If you've got the Big Four nailed down, rest assured that you're #winning. The next stage is to do a plastic audit (sounds super dull, actually quite interesting) and this is a great thing to do with your kids (from preschoolers upwards). The idea is that you collect all your plastic waste for a week, and then take a look at what's in there, because you can't change what you don't know. Here's how:

- If your kids are old enough, gather the family around (depending on how biddable your family are, this may be the hardest step) and introduce the idea. For top parenting points and all the smug feels you can also (attempt to) use this as an educational experience (there must be a Brownie badge or similar in it somewhere). Explain that you want to tackle how much plastic waste you're creating as a family and why you think it's important (obviously in an age appropriate manner). If your kids are keen, you could set them a project (again, in an age appropriate way) to research plastic pollution and some of the problems it causes.

- Find a box or old bin that you can use to house all your plastic waste for the week. Put it somewhere visible and again, if you're feeling keen, get the kids to design a label for it. Some people choose to put just their non-recyclable plastic waste in there, others put all their plastic, the choice is yours.
- For a week (if you can!) divert all your plastic rubbish from your landfill bin into the designated box.
- At the end of week, reconvene the family around the table and channel your inner rubbish detectives (dressing up as Sherlock Holmes is optional for this part). Take a look at what's inside the box. You can count the total number of items of packaging, or you can weigh it – anything to give you an idea of the total amount, and a baseline. If you've got older kids you can shoehorn all kinds of maths into this bit, making pie charts, bar charts, working out percentages etc. etc.
- Have a chat about your findings, and decide together which items you want to find alternatives for first. If you do it this way, the idea (may not work, but worth a go) is that you're more likely to get buy-in, rather than being the big meanie who bans Fruit Shoots. You never know, they might surprise you and come up with a plastic-free(ish) solution like only having them at weekends or special occasions (then again, they might not).

MICROFIBRES

We're all very aware now of plastic pollution in the oceans and the damage it is doing to wildlife and ecosystems. However, the plastic that we see floating around is only part of the story and scientists are becoming increasingly aware of the problems caused by microfibres. As the name suggests, these are teeny tiny fibres that are released from our clothes every time they're washed, which are too small to be filtered out at water treatment works and so make their way out into our water systems and then on into our oceans.

The vast majority of the clothes that we now wear are synthetic (i.e. man-made). Even knitted garments are often made from acrylic yarn which is made from oil. These tiny fibres are in fact microplastics, and are having a huge impact on aquatic ecosystems, and introducing plastic into our own food chains (*see* page 109 on glitter also).

Sadly there isn't yet a nice easy answer to this, but while we wait for washing machine manufacturers to catch on and introduce microfibre filters, there are a few things we can do:

- Look for clothes made from natural fibres wherever possible.
- Wash synthetic clothes, especially things like fleeces (which are one of the worst culprits for shedding) less often (anything that means less washing gets a thumbs up from me).
- Avoid tumble drying as much as possible – this makes the fibres more brittle and therefore more likely to shed.
- Have a look at something like a Guppyfriend washing bag (www. en.guppyfriend.com). This looks a bit like a large pillowcase, and the idea is that you put your synthetic fabrics in there, and the microfibres are then captured inside (you can then dispose of them in your normal landfill bin).

Getting the family on board

It's one thing deciding as an individual to make some changes to your lifestyle, it can be quite another persuading the rest of the family to join in. I know for a fact that if I decided to embark on a fitness regime, my chances of actually making any progress would be hampered significantly if I needed everyone else in my house to join in. I recently tried to get everyone excited about having a go at *Couch to 5K* and we didn't even get as far as donning trainers.

If your family are all lustily singing from the same song sheet, then that's amazing – please do skip this bit and proceed to the next section. Please also drop me a line to let me know how you've done it. Because although I'm going to share some ideas with you here, I'd be lying if I said that my whole family was as keen as I am to save the planet, and that we don't have arguments over buying kids' magazines festooned with instant landfill, and that we all gather around the TV every Saturday evening to watch an informative eco-documentary.

Mostly they're happy to go along with my ~~demands~~ suggestions, but sometimes it still feels really difficult to do the 'right' thing right now for their futures, when they basically just want to be doing all the same things as their friends. So if you're finding getting the family on board difficult, know that I feel your pain.

KIDS

The climate crisis is a huge, overwhelming, anxiety-inducing issue for us as grown-ups, so the challenge when talking to our kids about it is to explain the situation, and why we're wanting to make the changes we're making, without scaring the crap out of them.

I go into more detail for each age group in the appropriate chapter, but here are some key points to think about:

- **MEET THEM WHERE THEY ARE**
  Everything I've read (by people who are actually qualified in this kind of thing) says that it's important to 'meet kids where they are' and to talk about the climate crisis in a way that's understandable and accessible, which will obviously differ depending on their age.

  If they're asking questions, answer them as honestly as you can, but if they aren't really showing much interest, wait for them to come to it. Childhood is precious; we need to be really careful of projecting our own fears and anxieties onto them. Just because we're worried about it, and it's their future, doesn't mean they will be as invested in it as we are (or at all).

- **NURTURE A LOVE OF NATURE**
  Point out wildlife when you're out and about. Learn about our wonderful world and its inhabitants. We protect what we love.

- **KEEP THINGS LOCAL AND RELATABLE**
  It's really hard as adults to get our head around why us leaving our lights on is contributing to the melting of the polar ice caps, and even harder for kids. Talk about things that they can see: litter is a great one, and it's really easy to take action on by doing litter picks on your walks, or when you go to the beach.

- **LET THEM KNOW THEY ARE NOT ALONE**
  Talk about other children doing brilliant things for the planet, and the wonderful people and organisations around the world who are

working really hard to find solutions. If you see a good news story about the climate, share it with them – it's not all doom and gloom, even though it might feel like it at times.

- **FOCUS ON ACTION**

  This applies to us as adults as much as it does to our kids. I've found consistently that the antidote to eco-anxiety is eco-action. Brainstorm a list of things that you can do as a family, or that they can do themselves (obviously age dependent), and then pick ONE thing to do.

- **THINK ABOUT FORMING A FAMILY ECO-COMMITTEE**

  Many schools will now have their own eco-committees made up of pupils from across the year groups, and there's no reason why a similar set-up won't work at home, but with all the family members involved. Do a home audit of all the things you're already doing really well, and then a list of all the changes you still want to make. Get the whole family involved in this, and help to come up with ideas for what to focus on next and how to go about making the changes.

PARTNERS/SIGNIFICANT OTHERS

If you live with a partner this can be where it gets really tricky and frustrating (just in case it wasn't already). Maybe your partner doesn't appear to care, or is ambivalent, or thinks any changes are going to be expensive or take more time? Clearly the ideal scenario is to have our partners fully on board, supportive, and maybe even initiating some of the changes we're making as a household, and I'll share some ideas to make that so shortly. But even if that's not the case, it's not all bad news.

With a massive stereotyping klaxon type thing going off, in my experience it's the women in the family who take the lead on eco stuff (95+ per cent of my audience on social media are female), who worry about what's going on and are looking to make changes. In same-sex couples I've been told anecdotally that it can end up being the primary caregiver who takes on this role. Research by Mintel in 2015 found that mums make over 80 per cent of the buying decisions within households;

and when you couple that with the statistic on page 11 about 60 per cent of global greenhouse gas emissions coming from household consumption, it's easy to see that actually, mums hold a lot of power. Yes it's sexist, yes it's depressing that even in today's modern society it's still largely women who are burdened with looking after the home and caring for the kids, but let's also recognise that power, and the potential it brings to create positive change.

Having said all of that, although we might not actually need to have our partners on board, let's face it, it will make life easier if they are. When we did our year buying nothing new, my husband went along with my idea and plans in an 'anything for a quiet life' kind of way, hoping I would soon get distracted by another more exciting idea soon enough. Needless to say I didn't, and actually, once he realised quite how much money we were saving (I estimated a total of around £2000 over the year) he started to get a bit more excited about the whole thing. And that's OK – if your other half is more motivated by money saving than planet saving, run with it. It all has the same end result of lower consumption and therefore a lower carbon footprint.

Here are some additional tips for talking to your partner, if you have one:

1 TALK TO THEM ABOUT THE CHANGES YOU WANT TO MAKE

I tend to forget that my family aren't privy to my inner monologue (thank God) and get cross with them when they don't comply with my new rules when I haven't actually articulated my thought process. So it's actually not a surprise when they don't make the changes I've instigated in my head.

Confession: I unilaterally decided that we should start saving our crisp packets (yes, we still buy crisps) for the Terracycle scheme (https://www.terracycle.com/en-GB/brigades/crisppacket) and was annoyed when they kept on ending up in the bin. Took me a while to realise I hadn't actually told the rest of the family about my idea…

2 TALK TO THEM ABOUT HOW YOU'RE FEELING

Although awareness of the climate crisis is at an all-time high, at the time of writing it still doesn't feel like we're quite at the point where we're all having in-person conversations about this kind of stuff. I think there is a tendency to keep a lot of our eco-anxiety bottled up, or only to share on social media, so our partners might not actually be even all that aware of how we're feeling. If you're feeling really guilty and anxious every time you put a disposable nappy in the bin, have a chat with your partner about this, and see if they'd be up for trying some reusables.

3 ASK THEM WHAT THEIR CONCERNS ARE ABOUT MAKING SUSTAINABLE(ISH) CHANGES

Our brains are hard-wired to keep us safe, and to maintain the status quo. That means any change to 'normal', especially if it's unexpected or 'unprecedented', can feel really threatening and unsettling. If they're concerned about the cost of organic food for example, talk about some of the savings you'll be making in terms of food waste, or finding other things secondhand etc. It's not a given that any changes you make will take more time; some will be simple tweaks to your regular shopping list, or simply finding different places to buy the things you need.

4 BE PREPARED TO COMPROMISE

We tried and tried for ages with bar soap – in any article you read with 'top tips for being plastic-free' this is always touted as one of the easiest changes you can make. We tried it, we really really did. But my husband and the kids really didn't like it (and if I'm honest, I didn't either). So we looked for a compromise that everyone could get on board with – in this case, ordering 5L bottles of shower gel that we dispense into smaller bottles to use in the shower, and that double up as handwash and bubble bath. Not plastic-free, but plastic-free(ish) and at least the kids are actually washing their hands…

Confession: We use large refill bottles for shampoo too – I just can't find a shampoo bar that doesn't make my hair feel disgusting.

5 SHOW DON'T TELL

Sometimes the thought of change is worse than the change itself. Your partner might be worried about making the switch to reusable baby wipes because they've never seen them being used; they're worried about how much extra washing they'll generate, how effective they'll be, how you'll manage when you're out for the day etc. Probably all the things that you worried about before doing a spot of research (*see* page 72). Once you've got them, and started using them, they will pretty quickly see that they're actually super easy, AND you can point out the money you're saving on not buying endless packs of single-use wipes!

6 CHOOSE YOUR BATTLES!

Some changes you can make easily without your partner necessarily being any the wiser. If you do the supermarket shop, you can easily start buying loose fruit and veg, or more eco-friendly cleaning products. If you do the meal planning and cooking, sneak in some meat-free meals and see how long it takes them to notice. If there are changes that will affect them, or that you need them on board with, save the 'battles' for the ones that are really important to you.

7 REMEMBER THE 'ISH'

We've talked about compromise, and while that might be frustrating, remember that any change in the right direction is good. You might not be where you ultimately want to be straight away, and it might feel like two steps forwards and one back, but that's OK.

8 GO FOR A TRIAL PERIOD

Despite being the instigator of most of the sustainable(ish) changes in our household, I can see that being presented with a change as a *fait accompli* and something that you've got to 'like or lump' might have the potential to be a teeny bit antagonising. If it's a change that you think your partner might not be fully on board with (or that you know full well they're not fully on board with after a 'heated debate'), then suggesting a trial period can be a good compromise. For example, if you want the kids to get the bus to school rather than drive them, but maybe your partner is worried about logistics, or safety, or that the kids won't like it, could you try it for a month and then reassess? Set a timeframe that works for you both, and agree to come together at the end to decide on the way forwards.

9 ONE CHANGE AT A TIME

If we're a step or two ahead of our partners in our thinking about all things sustainable(ish), it can be tempting to want to make All The Changes, all at once. Forgetting that our newfound zeal and excitement around reducing single-use plastics or limiting food waste might not be shared, and might feel a little bit overwhelming for someone who was actually pretty happy with things as they were thank you very much.

If you can, create a plan together, decide on the changes you want to make first, and do them step by step. So you might have your eye on an electric car when you reach the point of replacing the skip you currently drive around in, but a great starting point is encouraging everyone to scoot to school, or get the bus into town rather than driving.

10 CELEBRATE YOUR SUCCESSES

If you're more organised than me, you might be able to track your spending and any savings you make, or the fact that you only need to put the bin out once a month rather than once a fortnight. This is useful as a tool for getting partners on board, but it's also really important for us – that we take a minute to give ourselves a pat on the back for how far we've come, rather than the usual human condition of berating ourselves for how far we've yet to go!

GRANDPARENTS AND RELATIVES

Sometimes you can feel like you're really nailing it – maybe your partner is on board (if you've got one) and if not actively instigating change, is at least complying(!), the kids are engaged and joining in, and you feel like you're really making some progress. And then there's a family occasion – a birthday, Christmas, a christening – and before you know it your house is filled with a baby elephant's worth of gifted plastic tat that you've had to accept while smiling through gritted teeth. It delights your kids for half a day and then you have to try and shoehorn it into your already bulging shelves and cupboards.

When my parents were alive, my mum was the worst offender for this – she just loved buying stuff for the kids. She'd spot things when she was out and about and buy them to give next time we saw her. And she'd go totally overboard at Christmas. In some ways, it was really lovely. It let us know that she was thinking about us and the kids, and it was her way of showing her love. But the more aware I became of the relationship between 'stuff' and the plight of the planet, the more difficult it became. Pushing back on people's gifts can very easily be seen as a rejection not just of the gift, but of their love. It's a real clash of values and I have to admit that I don't have any hard and fast answers (sorry).

It's also compounded by the fact that kids love presents (I think most adults love presents, too). The giddy excitement of Christmas and birthdays is due in no small part to the anticipation of lots of shiny new things to play with. Let's be honest, book vouchers and clothes, while nice, don't really cut the mustard. And it's hard to find that balance.

Confession: I usually spend November telling myself that the kids already have too many toys, that they really don't need anything, that we're going to be really sensible this year and assuring myself that they won't notice/mind a few less presents this year. And then spend December panicking that they haven't really got anything and they'll have nothing to open and will be really disappointed.

Creating positive change is hard. Working out ways to match up our actions with our values is hard. It can mean breaking habits that you've built up, often unintentionally, over a lifetime. And as discussed, it's hard enough getting our own immediate family on board. It can feel a hundred times harder to tackle these issues with the wider family. We're disrupting the family (and societal) status quo. It can feel like we're judging them (let's face it, we kind of are) and the choices they're making. It might feel like we're rejecting their love, and that we're ungrateful. Families are difficult beasts at the best of times, and we need to tread carefully and remember that c-word (compromise), remember that change doesn't happen overnight, and that relationships are what matters.

Here are a few ideas to try:

1 EXPLAIN WHERE YOU'RE AT

In the same way as your partner and kids aren't privy to your inner thoughts, your parents and in-laws aren't either. They also won't necessarily have seen the small, daily changes you've been making, so it can come as a real shock for you to suddenly turn around and announce that you only want them to, say, buy one present per child for Christmas. Drop into conversations some of the changes you've made. Tell them you're reading this book (or buy them *The Sustainable(ish) Living Guide* for Christmas!) and explain how it's made you really think about the some of the choices you're making. If you can, talk to them about your fears for the future of your kids, their grandkids. In an ideal world you'd be able to have a conversation with them, ahead of time, agree some boundaries and everyone would be happy. And if it were only that easy, I could stop right here...

2 BE PREPARED

When you get asked the question, 'What does little Tarquin want for his birthday?' even though your inner voice might be screaming, 'Nothing! There's nothing he needs, we have no more space to put anything else!' have a list at the ready of things that your small person will actually play with or needs. At least that way you won't end up having to find house room for some hideously large and unsuitable toy that is rarely even played with.

3 EXPERIMENT WITH SUGGESTING SOME GUIDELINES

For example, I know some families who have had 'secondhand only' rules for Christmas gifts. Or one gift per child. Or set a monetary limit. This obviously needs everyone to be in agreement though, otherwise this is where the clash of values can really be exacerbated. Even trickier if you have a wider family/siblings with kids who aren't on board.

4 BE SUPER SPECIFIC

Instead of saying 'clothes', point them to one of the ethical companies on page 80. Instead of saying 'Lego', or 'craft stuff' give them specifics of the set your child has been coveting, or the particular brand of craft stuff you'd prefer (*see* page 109). Encourage them to stick to the list!

5 SUGGEST EXPERIENCES OVER 'THINGS'

Christmas and birthdays can be overwhelming in terms of the volume of 'stuff' entering the house. One thing that's worked quite well for us in the past has been to make the suggestion that the grandparents take the kids for a day out later in the year – if they can do it with each child individually it allows for some really lovely 1:1 time for the kids. However, if they take them all at the same time, it allows you some really lovely 1:1 time on your own... Be warned though that some grandparents still feel the need to give them 'something little to open', so be ready for this and direct them accordingly!

6 GIFTS THAT KEEP ON GIVING

For the last couple of years my auntie has bought our eldest a subscription to the *Beano* for Christmas. He loves it, and gets the excitement of it dropping into the post box each week. There are a great range of kids' magazines and comics, and the bonus is that often with the subscription version, they don't come with all the plastic crap attached to the front (#winwin).

Something like a National Trust or English Heritage family membership makes a brilliant gift, and means you can have countless 'free' family days out all year. I will concede that opening a gift card membership for the National Trust might not be all that exciting for a five-year-old, but I'm also pretty sure that they'll have enough stuff to open from other people to not even notice. And maybe the grandparents could make a big thing of taking them for the first day out?

There are oodles of kids' subscription boxes for everything from arts and crafts, to science experiments, to gardening. Pick one that you think your child would love, and send the grandparents the link! Just make sure that it's something you think your kids will really love to receive each month though, otherwise it's just an added irritation of a monthly delivery of something else to find a home for that doesn't get used.

7 THIS LAST ONE WON'T BE FOR EVERYONE...

I know of some people who, frustrated after several years of having their pleas and suggestions ignored, have reached the point where they simply say outright that any unwanted/unasked for presents will be donated straight to the local charity shop. Like I said, not for everyone, and certainly not for me – I hate confrontation and would be far too scared!

Resources

- FREECYCLE (WWW.UK.FREECYCLE.ORG) AND FREEGLE (WWW.ILOVEFREEGLE.ORG)

  Free-to-use platforms with local groups where you can pass on your unwanted things to others, and also find things for free that you might need.

- LOVE FOOD HATE WASTE (WWW.LOVEFOODHATEWASTE.COM)

  Website with lots of ideas and recipes to help reduce food waste.

- GIKI EARTH (WWW.GIKI.EARTH)

  A great website/app that allows you to input your data and then calculates your carbon footprint. It then also sends you hints and tips for how to reduce it.

- *HOW BAD ARE BANANAS? THE CARBON FOOTPRINT OF EVERYTHING;*
  MIKE BERNERS-LEE, PROFILE BOOKS, 2020

  Easy book to dip in and out of with some interesting, and
  sometimes surprising, facts about the carbon footprint of pretty
  much everything.

2

Pre-baby

To **have a** baby or not is a huge decision, and it's one that's taken on a whole new context in the light of the climate crisis. Even when we were discussing it 11+ years ago before having our first, I distinctly remember having conversations with my husband around whether it was the 'right' thing to do given 'global warming' (as it was referred to then). Obviously we went ahead, and I can't now imagine life without our two growing boys, and the joy and laughter (and many, many sleepless nights) they have bought into our lives.

It's pretty safe to say that if you're reading this book, you either already have kids, have one on the way, or have made the decision that you want to. And I want to reassure you that there is no 'right or wrong' choice. Although all the information you might read, all the infographics and the charts, show that having 'one less child' is the most climate-friendly thing that you can do (how that even works I'm not sure? Does it mean if you were thinking about having just one, you don't have one, or only have two, even though you'd love a third?) what actually counts more than the number of children born, is how those children are raised. It doesn't take a scientist to work out that the carbon footprint of a child born in a rural community in the developing world will have a far smaller carbon footprint than a child born to one of the world's richest 1 per cent. It's not necessarily the number of children that's the problem, it's the volume of stuff that comes with each of them.

It's not my place, it's not anyone's place, to tell you whether or not to have children, or to tell you how many children to have, or to judge you for the decisions that you make. As we saw right back at the start of the book, how you raise your children has a huge impact on their carbon footprint, so let's focus on that.

Let's see how we can make a difference before our little bundle of sleep-depriving joy even makes an appearance.

PRE-PREGNANCY/PREGNANCY VITAMINS

NHS advice is to take folic acid if you're trying to conceive and for the first 12 weeks of pregnancy, as well as a vitamin D supplement during winter months. Whilst plastic might not be high on your mind in the first few months of pregnancy, especially if you're knackered and/or chucking your guts up, there are some plastic-free(ish) options out there:

- Wild Nutrition (www.wildnutrition.com) are a UK brand making high-quality supplements, supplied in glass jars with no plastic seal, and delivered in biodegradable packaging. They're also suitable for vegetarians.
- Plastic bottles are better than blister packs as they are widely recycled compared to the packs.

PREGNANCY TESTS

As soon as you see that line on the pregnancy test, your life changes. If you're reading this book, there's a pretty good chance you've already done your test, and are pregnant/already in charge of small people. So maybe this is food for thought for next time (if there is a next time!) or info to pass on to friends, but…

Have you ever thought about the amount of single-use plastic that goes into a pregnancy test? Nope, me neither until I started researching this book. But now I am thinking about it, I'm kind of freaked out. According to the Office for National Statistics, there were over 700,000 live births recorded in the UK in 2018. Even if we assume only one test per live birth, that's a LOT of plastic, isn't it? And plastic that ends up in landfill (unless you're weird like me and kept them because it felt somehow wrong to throw them away, but now I'm not really sure what to do with them… Just me?!).

Before I started researching this book I had no idea that there were plastic-free(ish) versions available, but there are! When you go to the doctors for a pregnancy test, there's no way the NHS can afford £15+

a pop for a pregnancy test, so what they use are little strip tests that you dip in some wee, and there's the line denoting a positive; it's just not encased in plastic. The good news is that you can buy these to use yourself, AND they're a huge amount cheaper #winwin.

Boots stock their own make at £5 for five strips, Poundland do two strips for £1, or you can find them online. I'm sure the strips probably come in plastic pouches, but it's still less plastic than a 'regular' test, and every little helps…

MATERNITY WEAR

Once you're safely through the first 12 weeks, thoughts are probably turning to maternity wear. If it's your first baby, you'll be desperate to start showing. If it's your second or more – first up, congrats if you've made it out of last time's maternity wear – you'll probably be despairing at how quickly your bump is showing. Either way, you might now be eyeing up elasticated waists.

Sadly, maternity wear hasn't escaped the 'fast fashion' makeover that the rest of the fashion industry has undergone in recent years, and low-quality, high-volume clothes are produced for pregnant woman in exactly the same way regular clothes are. Meaning that more often than not, people (the workers making these garments) and planet come way down the priority list for manufacturers and retailers.

It's sobering to think that one of the very first purchases we make as new parents could be having such a negative effect on both the health of mother earth, and the health of the women (over 80 per cent of garment workers are women) producing them.

Before you hit the shops, or ~~Google~~ Ecosia (*see* page 57) 'cheap maternity wear' remember to take a little look back at my very favourite buyerarchy of needs (*see* page 13) and see what planet friendlier options there might be.

USE WHAT YOU HAVE

First up, do you actually really need maternity wear yet?

Yes, I totally get it (especially if this is your first baby), buying maternity clothes is one of the very first 'I'm going to be a parent' things you get to do, and it's hugely exciting, and a very visible way of saying to the world 'Behold my child-carrying status'. But believe me when I say that you will very quickly tire of your maternity wardrobe, so putting off the point at which you have to embrace it might be something you end up being thankful for.

Have you got a pair of trousers lurking in your wardrobe that are a little on the baggy side? (Admittedly for most of us, the trousers lurking at the back of the wardrobe tend to be the ones that are a little on the tight side that we keep promising ourselves we'll fit into again…) Embrace your leggings with the stretchy waistband for as long as you can.

Waistband extenders are little loops that you can hook onto your buttons, and are an ingenious invention that allow you to keep wearing your normal trousers (as long as it's just your belly that's expanding and not the rest of you as you imbibe all the carbs…) for a little longer by giving you an extra bit of breathing room around the waist.

'Belly bands' are like boob tubes for your bump, and are another option that can be worn over your (un-buttoned) jeans and trousers to extend their life a little bit longer as you expand.

BORROW

Given that they're only used for a relatively short period of time, you might find that you have friends and family who are have maternity clothes they aren't wearing that they're happy to lend you. This option can be especially useful if you find yourself with a wedding or similar to go to whilst you're pregnant, and need a posh dress that you'll only wear once.

Maternity clothes rental services

I can't tell you how much I love this idea! I wish I'd known about it when I was pregnant – you pay a monthly subscription and get a certain number of maternity items delivered to your door.

- BELLES AND BABES (WWW.BELLESANDBABES.CO.UK/ MATERNITY)
  Choose from either the 'bespoke' (where they have a chat with you and then pick out items based on your style etc.) or 'ready to ship' services and get them delivered to your door to wear and return when you're bored of them/got too big for them.

- **BUNDLE 'N JOY (WWW.BUNDLENJOY.COM)**
  A maternity subscription service that sources quality pieces
  that can sustain long-term wear, meaning they can be rented
  out again and again. You can choose from everyday wear or
  'occasion pieces'.

- **GIRL MEETS DRESS (WWW.HIRE.GIRLMEETSDRESS.COM)**
  If you're just looking for a one-off outfit for a special occasion,
  Girl Meets Dress has a range of posh maternity frocks to hire for
  between two and seven days.

THRIFT

Buying secondhand maternity is a brilliant way to save some pennies,
and to simultaneously polish your eco-halo. Obviously check out all
the usual places like eBay, Gumtree and Preloved, and also the NCT
'nearly new' baby sales (have a look at www.nct.org.uk to find your
nearest sale).

The Maternity Wear Exchange (www.maternitywearexchange.
co.uk) is a UK-based dress agency for 'nearly new' maternity wear. You
can search for and buy secondhand clothes for your pregnancy, and also
sell on here once you no longer need them.

Baby showers

I'm aware of quite how old I'm going to sound when I say this, but 'back
in my day' I'm sure baby showers weren't even a thing. They seem to be
another American import that we have embraced with open arms, like
Black Friday and going bonkers about Halloween.

However, I'm given to understand now that they are very much
a thing and that it's no longer enough to allow expectant mothers to
simply waddle off on maternity leave clutching a card and a John Lewis
voucher. No, they must attend a 'surprise' baby shower with themed
cupcakes, bunting, balloons and the obligatory 'shower' of gifts.

Don't get me wrong, I have nothing against celebrating the excitement
around the imminent arrival of a shiny new person into the world, and
I'm sure that when they started, in the same way that wedding gifts were
originally intended, they were a really helpful way of making sure that

new parents had all they needed to welcome their child into the world. But this now seems to have morphed and (unsurprisingly) become hugely commercialised – I read a depressing article online recently talking about how to choose the right theme, the party games to play, and the goody bags for guests to take home.

Honestly, I'm not the fun police – I think it's really lovely to get friends and family together to celebrate this milestone, but all of this 'stuff', much of it single use, all has an impact on the planet and is maybe not the best way to usher a new life into the world.

So in the true style of 'sustainable(ish)', let's have a baby shower, let's come together with all those who want to wish us well, and offer their love and support, but let's think about ways we can do it in a slightly more planet-friendly manner.

In much the same way that the bridesmaids usually organise the hen do, I think it's usually understood that someone else will be in charge of the logistics of your baby shower. This being the case, you might want to have a chat with them beforehand about what kind of thing you'd like, or you could just pointedly leave this book lying around with a massive Post-it note arrow pointing to this page. (If you're unexpectedly thrown a surprise baby shower, accept that it was out of your control, and go with the flow.)

Much of the advice for kids' parties (*see* page 101) will also apply, but here are some more specific ideas and tips applicable to baby showers:

● SEND E-INVITES

Logistically easier, and people can add the event straight to their online calendar. If you want to do a 'proper' invite, look for recycled or FSC (Forest Stewardship Council) certified cards. Or how about some made from either recycled seed packets or plantable seed paper (the idea being that you plant the invite and it grows wildflowers – all the love for this idea!). Check out Wildflower Favours (www.wildflower-favours.co.uk).

● AVOID SINGLE-USE DECORATIONS

Balloons are a big no-no I'm afraid. Even though the rubber ones will 'biodegrade', it still takes years, and as we discovered on page 20, lots of stuff in landfill doesn't break down at all and just sits there for centuries to come. Possibly not the best way to welcome a new life into the world.

Paper pompoms can be carefully rescued after the event and reused for children's parties etc. It might actually be quite nice to have decorations that are pulled out year after year for the child's birthday celebrations that were originally used for their baby shower!

Bunting is another good one. If you've got a crafty friend, that could be their gift to you, especially if it's not too 'baby-ish' and can be reused on other occasions.

I'd love to claim this idea as my own, but I came across it in an article on baby showers – use small potted plants or succulents as decorations, and these can double up as little gifts for the guests to take home (should you feel the need). Genius!

● AVOID SINGLE-USE PLATES AND CUPS

One option is to ask guests to bring their own! This also saves on washing up too. If you're worried that you might get some strange reactions to this request, another possibility is to rent some vintage china for the occasion, or to see if you have a local party hire kit near you (*see* page 103).

● KEEP THE FOOD SIMPLE

Ask guests to contribute to the party food (I'm sure someone organised could create an amazing spreadsheet to make sure everyone brings something different). Homemade stuff obviously cuts down hugely on the amount of plastic packaging waste, but might depend on a) the catering skills of your shower organiser/ friends and b) how many people you've got coming.

● GIFTS

This is probably the big one. As we discussed on page 37, it's how we've come to show our love, and is ultimately what puts the 'shower' into baby shower. Without a little bit of input from you on what you need/would find helpful, there's a risk you could end up swamped with babygros and cute pairs of socks (that will never stay on) and possibly even a 'nappy bouquet' of disposable nappies when maybe you've got your heart set on having a go with reusables.

Either setting up a gift registry list, or asking for vouchers from your preferred store are good options that mean there's less risk of duplicates or being given things that you don't like! Or ask guests to contribute to a bigger item like the buggy or 'travel system' (bonus points for secondhand!).

Also, don't be embarrassed to actively encourage your guests to pass on any of their pre-loved baby stuff that they no longer use instead of gifts – they could attach a little label to their favourite babygro sharing a parenting hack they discovered, or a funny story about exploding poo…

There's more ideas in the 'new baby gifts' section on page 74 (on that note, what's the etiquette here? If you give a baby shower gift, does that mean you don't give a gift when the baby arrives? #confused).

What you need

When you're expecting a first baby, there are endless lists on the internet, telling you all the 'must have' items you need to buy before baby arrives. The insinuation being that you're a bad parent and not giving your precious bundle the best start in life if you don't buy all these things. But take a closer look – who produces most of these lists? I'm willing to bet that the majority are produced by retailers. Who want you to buy things. Ideally, their things. So what's the truth of it?

WHAT DO YOU REALLY NEED TO GET READY FOR WHEN BABY ARRIVES?

- SOMEWHERE FOR THE BABY TO SLEEP

  Most people will choose a Moses basket, but bear in mind that in Finland it's really common for new babies to sleep in a cardboard box (with a mattress). It's perfectly OK to use a secondhand Moses basket (however, please note the advice is to buy a new mattress for each baby – *see* page 17), and you might find that friends are only too keen to pass on theirs that has been sitting in the loft.

- SOMETHING FOR THE BABY TO WEAR

  Personally, I would try and resist the urge to dress your little one in mini versions of grown-up outfits. Yes, they look very cute, but they're a pain in the arse to change them in and out of, and more washing. Vests and babygros for the win. For added eco points, choose neutral colours so they can be used for any subsequent siblings, buy secondhand bundles, choose organic cotton, and/or use a rental service (*see* page 79).

● **NAPPIES**

Apparently some people do manage to rear their babies entirely without nappies (it's called 'elimination communication', check it out), however it's probably not a route that's going to be chosen by the majority of us. Nappies get their own special section (*see* page 61) but whether you choose disposables, reusables, or a mix, you will need some.

● **SOMETHING FOR THE BABY TO EAT**

Breast or bottle, the choice is yours, but whichever you choose, you'll need breast pads/nursing bras or formula and bottles and a way to sterilise them.

● **A CAR SEAT**

Even if you don't have a car of your own, there will probably be occasions when you travel in one (travelling home from hospital, on a day out with friends/parents etc.), so it's worth having a seat. It can also be another place to try and get the baby to sleep in when you're tearing your hair out (although bear in mind, the advice is not to let them sleep in there for prolonged periods).

● **A CHANGING BAG**

Or something to carry All The Things in when you eventually summon up the energy to leave the house. Remember that a rucksack you already have will do the job just as well!

● **MUSLINS**

All the muslins. These are the ultimate multipurpose things of wonder that you never even knew existed until you had a baby. They mop up all manner of spills, cover you up when you're attempting unsuccessfully to breastfeed discreetly, act as a sunshade hung over the buggy hood/car seat handle, double up as a bib when you've forgotten to pack one (again) and so much more. We still have some kicking around (our kids are 9 and 11!) and the kids use them at night when they've got snotty noses.

- **SOME WAY OF TRANSPORTING THE BABY**
  Whether that's a buggy, or a sling, or an all-singing, all-dancing 'travel system', you'll need some way of travelling with a small person in tow. More on this on page 54.

- **THERMOMETER**
  It came as a total surprise to us when we needed to know what the baby's temperature was – I don't think I had ever taken my own temperature before. Even if it's just to rule out a temperature as the reason for the non-stop wailing, this is a really useful piece of kit (and will continue to be so for many years).

WHAT YOU DON'T ABSOLUTELY NEED, BUT YOU MIGHT FIND USEFUL

- **A BABY MONITOR**
  I was unsure whether to put this in the must haves or not. It's one of the things we all rush out and buy, and possibly fear being judged if we choose not to buy one, but to be honest, unless you live in a mansion and the baby sleeps in the west wing, you WILL hear your baby crying. The only possible exception is if you're watching TV with the volume up, and then it's quite helpful to be able to see the lights flashing, rather than have to keep muting every 3 seconds when you think you might have heard a snuffle from the next room. For the first few months, the advice is that baby sleeps and naps in the same room as you anyway, so you could hold off and see how you get on?

- **A BOUNCY CHAIR THING**
  We borrowed one of these from friends and it was a godsend, just as another place to put them while you try and do a wee/cook tea/ do anything without a baby attached to you.

- **A BABY GYM THING**

  In all honesty, a towel would suffice, but you might find that the dangly bobbing about things distract your baby just for long enough for you to have a wee/cook tea/do anything without it all descending into tears (yours and theirs).

- **SPECIAL SHEETS FOR THE MOSES BASKET AND THE PRAM**

  These do in fairness make life easier as they're easy to take on and off, and they're guaranteed to fit properly, but you can just as easily cut up an old sheet to size (if you have the time/energy/inclination). Try to resist the urge to buy the elasticated fitted ones, as it's very hard to reuse these for anything else once the Moses basket is grown out of.

- **A CHANGING MAT**

  Although a folded-up towel will absolutely do the job, having something you can wipe clean is a godsend.

WHAT YOU DON'T NEED

Obviously, 'you do you'. Every pregnancy is different, every baby is different. You do what you need to do to get through. But these are some of the things that in hindsight I wish we hadn't bothered with. If you do want to try them out, see if you can find them secondhand, or borrow them from friends.

- **A VIDEO MONITOR**

  We actually never had one of these, but I don't think I need to see a video of my baby crying to know that it's crying. Maybe I'm wrong.

- **A BREATHING ALARM MAT**

  Again, we never had one of these, and I know from lots of people that they caused more stress by going off when the baby rolled off them, or something else set it off. Having said that, I think they may well be advised for babies with additional needs, so do take advice from your healthcare professional.

- **A 'YUMMY MUMMY' CHANGING BAG**

    In the same way that anything with the word 'wedding' in front
    of it automatically costs as least twice as much (cake, dress,
    stationery…), so does anything made specifically for new parents.
    It's entirely your choice, but I would urge you to resist anything
    overtly 'baby-ish' for your changing bag. Use a rucksack/bag you
    already have, or look for a good quality backpack with all the
    pockets (I do love a pocket).

- **A TOY SHOP'S WORTH OF BABY TOYS AND RATTLES**

    There is very little that your very young baby will play with.
    Most of them will end up dropping the toys on their own faces.
    And crying.

- **BABY CHANGING TABLE**

    Pop a changing mat on the bed (until baby can roll, then
    pop it on the floor). Simple. (Although if you've got a bad
    back, I will concede that this might save you a huge amount
    of back pain.)

I asked in my Facebook group which things people had bought for
their babies and never used – here's a selection:

- 'Swing seat – told by everyone it was magic to get baby to sleep.
  My son just screamed.' (Karen)
- 'I brought an on-the-go Milton dummy steriliser ball thing, never
  used it. I saw someone with one and they raved about it, but I
  found I just took a spare dummy out instead.' (Kathryn)
- 'This is going to be different for every family. We couldn't have
  done without our Moses basket and our baby hated the swing, but
  I know others who would have put them the opposite way around.
  My advice is get as much as you possibly can secondhand and re-
  gift it on when you're done with it.' (Sam)

With all the lists of 'must have things' that you'll be inundated with as
soon as you start perusing the interweb, again, remember the buyerarchy
(*see* page 13).

Borrowing can be your (not so) secret superpower for the early days, when babies are growing quickly and their developmental phases and needs change regularly. Asking friends if they've got stuff you can borrow can be really effective – if their baby is six months ahead of yours, but they're hanging on to stuff in expectation of a sibling, they're probably more than happy for you to borrow the Moses basket, the baby gym, the walker/bouncer etc. It saves them having to find space to store it, it saves you a shed load of money, and it's helping to save the planet too. It also gives you the chance to 'try before you buy' – allowing you to figure out whether you do actually need/want a baby monitor etc. What's not to love?

Baby transport

I very vividly remember standing, feeling very pregnant, with my husband in John Lewis staring in silent bewilderment at the vast array of different options on offer for buggies. Actually, not buggies, 'travel systems'. Oh my goodness. We were like rabbits in the headlights. Never had we anticipated that there would be So Many Choices. And that they would cost So Much Money!

There is a real pressure to choose the right ~~buggy~~ travel system. Is it compatible with the car seat that we'd already (it turns out rather foolishly and naively) bought, assuming that they would all work with any buggy? Does it come with a carry cot? Does the buggy bit face forwards? If it doesn't, am I scuppering my child's chances of getting into Oxbridge by denying them eye contact during our walks to the shops? Will it even fit in the car…?

Or do we actually want a sling?

Or both?

Argggghhhhhhhh!!!!

It can feel like a monumental decision – one of the first really big decisions of our parenting lives. And just before I make you feel better about it (*see* opposite) I'm going to turn the screw a little. Bear in mind that you're not only potentially wasting a good chunk of your monthly pay cheque by choosing a buggy that you end up hating, or that just isn't quite right, there's also a shed load (technical term) of resources and plastic in a travel system, and it comes with a pretty hefty carbon footprint.

So what are your lower-pressure, lower-impact (lower-cost) options?

ASK YOUR FRIENDS

Everyone who's recently had kids will have an opinion on what you'll need, and it can be worth listening to the pros and cons of the buggy they settled on. (Those without kids will look at you blankly and wonder why this is causing you such angst. They have no idea.) They might also have one stashed in the garage while they're in-between babies that you can borrow to see how you get on with it.

BUY ONE SECONDHAND

There's still the risk of it not being The One, but a. (whisper it) there is no perfect pram, and b. you will have saved some money, as well as the resources that would have been used to make a brand new buggy.

RENT

Buggi (www.buggi.co.uk) is 'the UK's first affordable, flexible and sustainable buggy leasing service'. You pay a monthly fee to rent a buggy, and if it turns out it's not the one for you, you can return it and pick another. I wish this had been around when ours were little.

SLING LIBRARIES

I found a sling indispensable with both of ours, and especially with number two. It meant I could just strap them in and get on with cooking, playing with a toddler etc., without (or at least with less) constant grizzling from a baby who wants to be held. As with buggies, there are a bewildering array of slings, from the simplest wrap slings that you can make yourself from a length of fabric (if you're dextrous enough to master the whole wrapping thing without dropping the baby), through to eye-wateringly expensive all-singing all-dancing models that practically carry the baby for you. Have a look to see if you have a 'sling library' near you – you could ask your local NCT group if they know of any, or do a quick ~~Google~~ Ecosia search. These work like regular libraries and let you borrow a selection of slings for a period so you can try before you buy.

Hospital bags

A quick word on single-use items in your hospital bag. You will find endless lists in baby books and online detailing everything you 'must have' in your hospital bag. I'm not even going to try and tell you what to take with you, but there are a couple of things I want to say here.

Nappies will take over your life very quickly, and even though you might have already decided (after reading the nappy section in here on page 61) what route you want to go down when it comes to reusables/disposables, if you need permission to cut yourself some slack when you and your new baby are in hospital (if you have a hospital birth) then here it is. I'm sure that some people do manage it, especially with second and subsequent babies, but if thinking about attempting reusable nappies in hospital with your newborn is making you feel anxious (it would me) don't do it. You will be knackered, you will be overwhelmed, and if you're the one who has given birth, your hormones will be all over the place and you will be feeling a bit bruised and battered. Now is not the time to start beating yourself with the eco-stick. Remember this is *The Sustainable*(**ish**) *Guide to Green-Parenting*, **not** *The Perfectly Sustainable Greener than Green Guide to Green-Parenting*. Grab yourself a pack of newborn nappies and pop them in your bag. It's one less thing to worry about, and if you want to try reusables, you can do that in the relative quiet of your home, once you feel up to it, and with the support of your partner (if you have one) to help you muddle through the first few nappy changes.

Having said that, do avoid disposable paper pants. I'm happy to say I've never used them, and never felt the need. A big pair or two of comfy washable pants will suffice.

If you've had a vaginal birth, you will need some form of gigantic sanitary towel to soak up your post-partum bleeding. The good news is that you don't have to go down the disposable route here (although again, you might want to while you're in hospital – if you do, that's absolutely OK). Reusable sanitary towels are now widely available online and many of them will do a 'super mega' version for either super heavy periods or for use after giving birth. Wear 'em out pads (www.wearemout.co.uk) are a brilliant independent British brand and have a 'Mega-Mega Flo' pad that you can buy individually, in a pack of six or as part of a 'post birth gift box' which also contains all kinds of lovely goodies for new mums.

And if you need a bag (or seven) of plastic-wrapped jelly babies to sustain you while you push out an actual human being, whack them in your bag (and try not to scoff them before you actually start to give birth). In this situation you do whatever you need to do to get through.

5 QUICK WINS FROM YOUR SOFA DURING MATERNITY LEAVE

I'm told that there are some people who use their maternity leave to 'nest' – they clean the whole house from top to bottom, get the freezer prepped with wholesome and nutritious homemade meals ready for when the baby arrives, and do all kinds of other things to get ahead and prepare. There are others (me) who feel like they *should* spend their time doing those things, but instead end up on the sofa binge watching Netflix and feeling guilty for having no kind of nesting instinct whatsoever.

Whichever category you fall into, and indeed anywhere in between, there are some general 'good eco' things you can do, from the comfort of your sofa, whilst you gestate. Many of them can even be fitted into an ad break. These aren't specifically parenting related, but are easy things you can do that will allow you to slash your carbon footprint and feel smug, and are the kinds of things you're unlikely to have the time/headspace to do once your little bundle of joy arrives.

1 **Switch your search engine to Ecosia** There's every chance that you might be online a LOT in the coming months, scrolling through your phone during seemingly endless night feeds. Why not use the power of your internet search to plant some trees! Ecosia (www.ecosia.org) is an alternative to Google that plants trees when you search. Its tree planting saves more CO_2 than it uses, and it's funding some brilliant tree planting projects all around the globe. There's an app you can install on your phone, and you can also use it on your laptop/desktop too. I can't remember how many searches you need to fund a tree being planted, but it's really not that many – I've 'planted' nearly 50 so far on my mobile alone!

2 Switch your gas and electricity to a green tariff
This is one of those jobs we put off, isn't it? It feels like it will be super complicated, time consuming, and is incredibly dull and grown up. BUT what if I were to tell you that it could save you money, will take less than 10 minutes, could slash your carbon footprint by up to a quarter (if you choose renewable electricity and carbon offset gas), AND can be done from your sofa? Big Clean Switch (www.bigcleanswitch.org) is an energy comparison site that only lists renewable tariffs – grab a recent bill (so that you can get an accurate quote), head on over to the website and you'll be done before the kettle's boiled.

3 Move your money
If you're in a switching mood, run with it, and look into switching your finances to ethical choices too. Triodos (www.triodos.co.uk) has an ethical current account, and has a seven-day current account switch guarantee, which means that they do all the work of switching all your direct debits etc. Don't forget to also look at any savings and investments you might have, including your pension. Good with Money (www.good-with-money.com) is a brilliant website to check out with stacks of info about the growing array of ethical investment choices, so that your money is working as hard for the planet as you are.

4 Join your local Freecycle/Freegle group
Have a look on www.ilovefreegle.org to find your local group. I live in a fairly small market town, and we have a group, so I reckon you're pretty likely to have one near you. Join up and take a look at what's on offer. Remember that you can post 'WANTEDS' if there's a particular thing you're looking for, e.g. size eight wellies for your toddler as you need a pair to leave at pre-school. And don't forget to use it to offer up any of your stuff if/when you have a declutter!

5 Share the changes you're making with friends and family
When we hear the word 'activism', I think most of us think of Greta, and Extinction Rebellion, and may well quail at the thought of having to get shouty with a placard. But I strongly believe

that we all have the potential to be 'everyday activists' through the different choices we make every day. Those choices are in themselves powerful – we're voting with our money and letting businesses know what kind of world we want. And even better, we can amplify the impact of those choices by sharing them with our friends and family, whether that's in person or on social media. The more visible we make these changes, the more 'normal' they become. Friends might see your Facebook post and think, 'Oh, if Susan can do it, maybe I'll have a go too.' Embrace your inner activist. From the sofa.

Over to you

When you're pregnant, there's a lot of focus on your birth plan. But what about your 'post-birth plan'? Could you use some of the time before your baby arrives (if you don't have a toddler/older child demanding your time!) to make a plan for what kinds of things you'd like to use or do once they are here?

In the same way that a birth plan might go out of the window in the heat of the moment, your post-birth plan might not be something you stick to rigidly, especially in the first months. But it gives you some intentions. And once you're a bit more settled into your new role as a parent, you can use it to remind yourself of the eco-bits you wanted to embrace before your life got turned upside down.

Brainstorm a few ideas and list them below:

Action	Timeframe
1.	
2.	
3.	
4.	

Resources

- **NATIONAL CHILDBIRTH TRUST (NCT) (WWW.NCT.ORG.UK)**
  National website with lots of information for new and expectant parents, including details of 'nearly new' sales.

- **UK NAPPY NETWORK (WWW.UKNAPPYNETWORK.ORG)**
  Find your nearest nappy library using their directory.

- **SLING PAGES (WWW.SLINGPAGES.CO.UK)**
  UK directory of sling libraries.

- **BIG CLEAN SWITCH (WWW.BIGCLEANSWITCH.ORG)**
  An energy comparison site that only lists renewable tariffs.

- **ECOSIA (WWW.ECOSIA.ORG)**
  Search engine that uses its advertising revenue to plant trees.

- **GOOD WITH MONEY (WWW.GOOD-WITH-MONEY.COM)**
  A great website with stacks of advice on how to make sure your money is doing as much good as you are.

- **SWITCH IT (WWW.SWITCHIT.MONEY)**
  Check out how well or otherwise your current bank and energy provider perform when it comes to the planet.

- **MAKE MY MONEY MATTER (WWW.MAKEMYMONEYMATTER.CO.UK)**
  A campaign and website to help you find out what your pension might be funding (it could be fossil fuels and arms…) and how you can demand a pension you can be proud of.

New baby

Holding **your new** baby in your arms for the very first time is amazing. There's no doubt about it. But there's also very little doubt that at least one of you will be tired, emotional, tired, overwhelmed, and tired.

You're experiencing a crash course in doing 'unprecedented things'. Many new parents have never changed a nappy before, let alone fed a baby and kept it alive. This is not the time to be holding yourself up to some kind of green parenting ideal. You do what you need to do to get through these early days. No judgement, no guilt.

We were the proverbial rabbits in the headlights with our first. Obsessed with getting him to feed, attempting to get him to sleep, how many nappy changes a day, should we bath him, shouldn't we bath him, why the hell won't he sleep…

If you need to survive on ready meals, get an online shop that comes encased in plastic bags, and are going through disposable nappies at a rate of knots, don't sweat it. The time WILL come when you can lift your head up, breathe, and start to make more informed decisions. And once you start to feel a bit like you can think and function, then you can start to think about any changes you might like to make, baby step (pun intended) by baby step.

Nappies

I'm sure whole books could be written just on this very subject, but I'll do my best to précis the pertinent info here, because we're all busy, and some of us have got nappies to change…

- Around three billion nappies are thrown away each year in the UK.
- Disposable nappies account for 2–3 per cent of all household waste.
- By the time they're potty trained the average baby will have used 4000–6000 disposable nappies, or 20–30 reusable ones.
- Reusable nappies can save parents between £200–500 over the course of a child's nappy wearing time, and even more if they're used for subsequent children. Although clearly there is a significant initial outlay needed for reusables.
- By using real nappies, the average household waste of families with babies can be halved!
- Around 25 per cent of a disposable nappy is plastic.
- Disposable nappies use up to three and half times more energy to make than reusable nappies.

So it's pretty clear that disposable nappies are not 'that great' for the planet. But we're all about the 'ish' here, so let's explore some options and the pros and cons of each.

First up, remember that *none of the choices you make have to be all or nothing.* We found that neither of our boys got on with reusable nappies at night (ending up with sore willies – TMI?) so after trying loads of different options and much angst, we decided to use disposables at night time. I confess I did feel like a bit of a failure, but now I'm older and wiser and have embraced the 'ish', I'm here to tell you that that's a load of old bollocks. Every reusable nappy used is one less in landfill. So using disposables at night means 7 nappies a week in landfill, but that's still better than 35 nappies a week in landfill if we were using them all the time.

Do what works for you.
Make the best choices you can as often as you can,
and don't beat yourself up.

Confession: After a week away in a self-catering cottage attempting to wash and dry nappies, we quickly decided a holiday felt more like a holiday if we used disposable nappies while we were away.

DISPOSABLE NAPPIES

Single-use nappies get a bad rap when it comes to the planet, for the reasons listed above, but they aren't all bad. Can you imagine the joy on the faces of mothers when they were first invented – no more hours spent slaving over the washing machine, no more drying nappies draped over every surface in the house, no more wrangling recalcitrant toddlers into stiff terry towelling and accidentally sticking them with a nappy pin. It must have felt like a revolution!

PROS

- They're super convenient.
- They're widely available – you can pick them up in your supermarket shop or at your local chemist.
- Unused ones are neat, small and light to carry.
- No extra washing and drying to be done.
- The easiest option for most childcare settings.

CONS

- They use a lot of raw materials, including plastic.
- They're single use, so all of the carbon and water that has gone into making and transporting them is wasted as soon as they are disposed.
- They take hundreds of years to break down when you throw them away, so a nappy that has been used for just a couple of hours (or less if you misjudge the timing of a nappy change – why is it that babies seem to love poo-ing in a nice clean fresh nappy?!) will be hanging around for centuries to come.
- In landfill, they contribute to the generation of greenhouse gases, such as methane, contributing to the climate crisis.
- We get through a LOT of them, potentially doubling the waste we're sending to landfill whilst our child is in nappies.

I'm sure I read somewhere that if Jane Austen had worn disposable nappies, we'd still be finding them in landfill (and probably making a fortune flogging them on eBay). And it's not just the emissions they create when they're thrown 'away'. Plastic is made from oil. A fossil fuel.

We need the oil to stay in the ground if we're to have any chance of keeping global temperature rises below 1.5°C (the figure we need to keep below to avoid the worst effects of climate change), so the less virgin plastic we're using, the better.

HOW ABOUT 'ECO' AND 'BIODEGRADABLE' NAPPIES (AND ALSO NAPPY SACKS, WIPES ETC.)?

I'm in two minds about these. On the one hand, it's easy to dismiss them as a whole heap of greenwashing (making misleading claims that make something appear greener than it actually is). Invented by clever marketing types who have recognised the guilt that many of us feel about using disposable nappies, and exploited that to create what seems like the perfect solution – all the convenience of disposables without the impact.

As we discovered on page 20, even eminently biodegradable things like newspapers can still be dug up from landfill sites relatively unchanged after 30-odd years. So regardless of whether your nappy claims to 'biodegrade' in 20 years or 300, it might actually not really make that much of a difference. And the term 'biodegrade' is open to a lot of misinterpretation…

When we read that something is biodegradable, I think most of us assume that it means that the item will break down pretty quickly into natural and innocuous substances – that it kind of composts and becomes new soil. Sadly, more often than not, that's not the case and it's a term that doesn't really have any regulation around its use. Many of these items need high temperatures, and/or oxygen to decompose, and they don't get these conditions in landfill. What is more likely to happen is that instead of 'breaking down', they 'break up' and fragment into smaller and smaller particles of microplastics, which are then much more likely to enter ecosystems and food chains.

But it's not all bad news and greenwashing. Many of the 'eco' brands of nappies use more sustainably sourced materials, and have less plastic in them than conventional ones, so they probably have a lower impact in their production, even if they don't break down any quicker in landfill.

NAPPY RECYCLING

I had no idea this was even a thing before I started to do a little digging around for this book, but it is! It sounds pretty grim, doesn't it? But apparently it's possible to recycle soiled nappies and incontinence pads. I'm not entirely sure of the magic that is involved (and not too sure I want to delve into it too deeply to be honest) but the recycling process involves harvesting the cellulose (the absorbent bit) and plastic (presumably minus poo) into things like construction cladding. Sadly it appears at the time of writing that this service (from www.nappicycle. co.uk) is only available across Wales – where they work with seven local authorities and process over 800,000 nappies a week. But it's really heartening to know that it can be done!

COMPOSTING YOUR NAPPIES

Yes, apparently this is a thing.

Obviously you need to use 'biodegradable' nappies. I have heard of people who have done this successfully, but you need a pretty high heat, and I shudder to think of the size of compost heap you would need to deal with a baby's worth of nappies… Catherine is in my Facebook group and she did it when her kids were young:'I had probably around 4 daleks (a type of compost bin) but these will have been well managed – hot, turned and plenty of other material in there too.'

I think if you're not already a confident composter with plenty of bins, this might be something to leave to those who are!

REUSABLE NAPPIES

This is where your head might start to hurt. In the same way that you might have felt overwhelmed by pram options, modern reusable nappies have the potential to do the same. No longer simply consisting of terry towelling wraps, massive nappy pins that would never pass modern health and safety standards, and sweaty plastic covers, there is now a potentially bewildering array of options available. There are:

- All-in-ones that look like 'regular' nappies and have removable inserts you pop into a pocket or popper in.
- Birth-to-potty that will fit from newborn to potty training through the clever use of poppers that adjust the size.

- Two-parters, where you have an absorbent nappy and then a separate waterproof liner.
- And more…

They can be made of bamboo, microfibre, cotton, hemp. You can have poppers or Velcro for fastenings. You can choose from a wide range of larger companies, or buy from a WAHM (work at home mum) making their own bespoke range. It's like Pinterest for nappies – a huge rabbit hole of stuff you never even knew existed, but suddenly you want to try them all…

As ever, there are pros and cons to the different types of nappy and the materials that they are made from. Bamboo and hemp are kinder to the planet in their production and tend to be very absorbent, but because of their absorbency they can take an age to dry. Microfibre nappies and inserts dry very quickly but are synthetic and as the name implies, are made up of teeny tiny fibres, usually plastic, that can shed into the water system when washed (*see* page 29). Obviously this isn't ideal, and currently until washing machine manufacturers catch up and start installing microfibre filters, it is a case of trying to find that balance between synthetic fibres and drying times.

Traditional cotton is a very water- and pesticide-hungry crop to grow. Organic cotton does better on the water and pesticide front but can be slow drying. GAH!!

The 'nappy system' (type of reusable nappies) that you choose should be based on weighing up different factors – age and size of your baby, how much they wee (you can boost the absorbency with extra inserts if you have a big wee-er), drying time you can manage, aesthetics (some people love showing off their 'cloth bums'), personal choice and probably a whole lot more. Although it's incredible to see the huge range of choices available to parents now – so many more than since my kids were tiny – I do think there's a tendency for new parents looking into reusables for the first time to find it all too much, too confusing, and to understandably retreat back to the familiarity and convenience of disposables.

A real life, real nappy experience from Elizabeth.

With my first, I'll be honest, neither myself nor my husband had any clue of anything "baby". We signed up for NCT classes and they gave us a demo of changing disposable nappies and we got some free samples. When number one came along we used them, and given no nappy rash occurred, we stuck loyally to the same brand for three years.

When baby number two arrived, I was far more environmentally aware and open to alternatives, but I just hadn't got round to researching options and didn't know where to start. But seeing the mountain of smelly plastic mount up in my bin, I was delighted when Jen suggested a nappy library near to me. I'd used a "sling library" before and credit it in saving me a fortune in bad purchases with the team's experience and the option to try before you buy, and the nappy library seemed to work in a similar fashion.

I got in touch and within 30 minutes of visiting them, I was good to go with a starter pack containing a selection of brands. This pack has lasted me five months, as they are more flexible to grow with your baby than disposables. There's one style in the kit I like to use more than the others, so I am looking to buy that for the next stage, with the intention of donating to the library after use as they are increasingly short on kits with growing demand.

I confess, I do still use disposables at night and when out and about (so have switched to a more sustainable brand), but I love to see my baby in her favourite "fuzzy knickers" which are so snug.

I definitely recommend to any new parents to find a library near them (ideally before baby arrives when you have more time) as they'll be out of them again before you know it!

TRY BEFORE YOU BUY

Here's a few ways to dip your toe in and have a try before you invest in a whole stash of nappies:

Look to see if you have a local nappy library near you

Nappy Libraries allow you to borrow a set of nappies, sometimes for a small charge, often for free, so that you can try them out. And many will have volunteers who will help you to get your head around what will work for you, and walk you through washing them. There's a map of UK nappy libraries on the UK Nappy Network website (www. uknappynetwork.org) – take a look.

Ask a friend

Even if none of your friends use cloth nappies, you might bump into someone at a baby or toddler group who does. Ask them if they wouldn't mind showing you the ropes – be brave! They will almost certainly be uber keen to show off their nappy stash and to recruit another member to the cause.

Try secondhand first

It might seem slightly weird to think that there's a market in secondhand reusable nappies, but there is, and it's huge! Sometimes people will try a nappy and not really get on with it, or there are some people who seem to become slightly addicted to amassing reusable nappies (not something to be recommended for sustainable(ish) purposes!), and have to have regular 'de-stashes' to keep their collection under control. There are loads of Facebook groups and forums online, many with selling pages, and it can be a great way to try out a particular make of nappy for a lower price.

Washing reusable nappies

A lifecycle assessment study for the global warming impact of disposable and reusable nappies produced by DEFRA in 2008 found that how reusable nappies are laundered has a significant impact on their overall carbon footprint.

Washing nappies on a full load, line drying, and reusing nappies on a second child (you can pass them on to another family if you don't have a second child) saves over 200kg of CO_2 (compared to the baseline of 'average' washer and dryer use) over two and a half years (equal to driving a car 1000km). Washing at 90 °C and tumble drying all the time pumps out an additional 420kg of CO_2 over the two and half years compared to the baseline.

The advice given in the conclusion for cloth nappy users to reduce their environmental impacts is to:

- Line dry outside whenever possible.
- Tumble dry as little as possible.
- When replacing appliances, choosing more energy efficient appliances (A+ rated machines are preferred).
- Not wash above 60°C.
- Wash fuller loads.
- Reuse nappies on other children.

HOW TO WASH REUSABLE NAPPIES

1   Take the nappy off (important step).
2   Shake/scrape/'plop' off any poo down the toilet.
3   Take out any inserts if you have 'all in one' or 'pocket' nappies, and do the nappy back up again (this stops the Velcro strips all getting tangled up with each other, and you ending up with a giant nappy ball in the machine) and turn the nappy inside out.
4   Pop the dirty nappy into your dirty nappy storage system. The traditional advice used to be to soak nappies in a nappy bucket before washing, however this is no longer the case. Ideally you shouldn't leave your nappies sitting in the nappy bucket for any longer than two days before washing (i.e. do a nappy wash every other day). If you do this you shouldn't really get any smell from the bucket. We used one of those mini dustbins that look like an actual dustbin but are about a quarter of the size, which we already had kicking around in the garage. And we used to put a muslin at the bottom of the bucket with a couple of drops of essential oil on it to help mask any smells. If you can, find a net laundry bag that fits into your nappy bucket,

then you can lift the whole thing out and chuck it into the machine. Otherwise, you may want to designate a rubber glove as the 'nappy glove' and leave it by the washing machine...

5   Do a rinse or pre-wash cycle.

6   Official advice is to wash at 60°C to kill any bugs that might be lurking in baby poo, but I tend to think that if your baby has a bug, you're all going to get it, regardless of the temperature you wash your nappies at. Most nappy experts now say to wash at 40°C, which is obviously more environmentally friendly.

7   Run a full wash at 40°C. Resist the urge to use the ECO cycle, as in this case we want the extra water to rinse things out thoroughly.

8   Check with the nappy manufacturer whether they recommend bio or non-bio washing detergent – most will recommend non-bio.

9   AVOID fabric softener – this builds up on the nappies and reduces their absorbency.

10 Higher spin speeds mean shorter drying times, but don't go too crazy as very high spin speeds may damage your nappies.

11 Air drying outside on the washing line is the gold standard if you can. Sunlight is the best for getting poo stains out (this applies to babygros and vests that have been caught up in poo explosions too). Using a free-standing dryer indoors is a good next best, but will take longer. Avoid hanging directly on radiators as it can make them go quite crunchy and can damage some delicate fabrics like bamboo. Tumble drying is OK if you have to, but obviously negates the eco impact a little, and can reduce the longevity of your nappies.

If all of that feels like a bit much, have a look to see if there are any nappy laundering services near you. I have to confess to not having much luck when searching online (I found one in London) but it's definitely worth asking your local NCT group to see if they know of any.

Nappy accessories

NAPPY LINERS

These go inside your reusable nappy, and in an ideal world catch all the poo, so that your actual nappy doesn't get covered in it. You can get disposable ones, or reusable ones, and as ever the choice is yours. One important thing to note though: unless specifically labelled as 'safe to flush' please don't flush your disposable liners down the loo. They cause blockages and contribute to the 'fatbergs' that we sometimes see horrendous pics of on social media. They should go in the bin.

NAPPY CREAM

Regardless of what you use, I would say (in my totally unprofessional opinion) that it's incredibly rare for a baby to get through nappyhood without at least a couple of bouts of nappy rash.

- Earth Conscious (www.earthconscious.co.uk) do a vegan and plastic-free baby balm that comes in a stainless steel tin (and also doubles up brilliantly as hand moisturiser!).

- Pure Nuff Stuff (www.purenuffstuff.co.uk) do a 'bum balm' (which I think I would buy just on the name alone) that also comes in a stainless steel tin with two sizes: 120ml to keep at home, and a handy 30ml one to keep in your changing bag.

BABY WIPES

Wet wipes literally didn't exist until the 1970s but now they seem to have become synonymous with parenting, and in the UK we use over 10.8 billion a year – that equates to 38,000 wipes each, over our lifetimes.

And they're not just for nappy changes; the wipes companies have cottoned on to our love of convenience and expanded their market (and profits) with wipes for cleaning the kitchen, the bathroom, the loo. Wipes to use when you've been to the loo, anti-bacterial wipes … you name it, there's a wipe for it.

When our kids were little, even though we were using reusable nappies and wipes for mucky bums, we still had the ubiquitous packs of wipes in the changing bag, upstairs, on the kitchen counter, in the car… They're just so bloody useful aren't they? But they're also a bloody nightmare for the planet. Sorry.

While I think many of us might assume that wipes are paper based (if indeed we think about it at all), the vast majority are in fact made of plastic. And plastic is made from oil. So it's a double whammy for the planet – using up fossil fuels to create single-use products that don't break down when they're thrown away. Add to that the fact that if they're flushed they block sewers, they can end up in the sea. In 2015, the Marine Conservation Society released data showing a 400 per cent rise in wipes found on beaches. I would imagine that has only continued to rise since then.

All in all not good.

So what can we use instead?

Reusable wipes

If you're already using reusable nappies, then reusable wipes are kind of a no-brainer. And even if you're not using reusable nappies, reusable wipes for nappy changes are way easier than you might think.

Cheeky wipes (www.cheekywipes.com) have a great reusable wipes kit for nappy changes that includes the wipes, 'clean' and 'dirty' boxes plus essential oils. It's really easy to set up and use, and a great easy first step into all things reusable. Old flannels or cut-up bits of towel will also do the job just as well.

If you're not sure about using them for nappy changes, try popping a box in the kitchen to use at meal-times for messy hands and faces to start with (and just chuck them straight into the washing machine). Or simply use a good old flannel.

Remember also that it doesn't have to be all or nothing – start off using your reusable wipes at home, and then if you want to you can 'graduate' to taking them out and about with you. There are all kinds of snazzy waterproof wipes bags available, including some that have separate clean and dirty compartments.

I distinctly remember deciding to go 'cold turkey' on baby wipes during our year buying nothing new and being pretty daunted by the prospect. But I promise you, it was far easier than I thought it was going to be. Yes, the kids might have ended up a little bit grubbier than they otherwise might have done, but it's all good stuff for their immune systems (that's my very scientific justification…!).

'Biodegradable' and 'flushable' wipes

As with all many things labelled as 'green' it pays to do a little bit of digging before you take it at face value. Wipes should categorically NOT be flushed – even wipes labelled as 'flushable' fail to meet the water industry's disintegration tests. Water UK have created a 'fine to flush' certification for any wipes that **do** pass the disintegration tests, and so far (at the time of writing) the only wipes that have passed the test are the 'Moist Tissues' from Natracare.

It's probably a good time to say it again – it's **not** all or nothing. Wipes are a life-saver for many of us, and the wet wipe police aren't going to come beating your door down if you pop a couple of packs in your weekly shop. But remember the waste hierarchy? Can you incorporate a little bit of reduce and reuse into your wet wipe usage? Every disposable wipe not used is one less in landfill, or ending up on our beaches.

Could you use reusables at home?

Could you aim to halve your use of disposable wipes?

What feels like a do-able challenge for you and your family?

New baby gifts

A new baby is cause for celebration and many of us want to show our excitement and pleasure for the new family with a gift. And, as with baby showers, this can result in an influx of presents that may never actually end up being used. Here are a few alternative suggestions if you're looking for a gift for a new arrival and their parents, or if people are asking you for ideas:

- **COOK A MEAL**
  Or better yet, set up a meal train (www.mealtrain.com). This is such a brilliant idea, I wish I'd known about it years ago. It's a website where you can create an interactive calendar and invite friends and family who then fill in the slots with meals that they make and drop round to the new parents' house. Literally a train of home-cooked meals arriving at your door, just when you need it most.

- **PATCHWORK (WWW.PATCHWORKIT.COM)**
  Another brilliant idea! You set up a 'patchwork' of things that will be useful for you: e.g. an hour's babysitting; doing some ironing; popping on a load of washing; taking the older kids out for a couple of hours.

- **ASK FOR SECONDHAND GIFTS**
  Ask friends if they can lend you their 0–3 month baby clothes, pass on their child's favourite book or toy they've outgrown.

- **SLEEP!**
  I know you can't really gift new parents sleep, but could you offer to take the new precious bundle out for a walk in the pram for an hour after they've been fed so that they might get the chance of a hot cuppa and a sit down?

- **ANYTHING SWEET AND CALORIFIC**
  Bake a cake, some brownies, or a batch of biscuits. I guarantee you will be greeted with open arms from even the most die-hard sugar refuse-niks.

Ethical savings accounts/ISAs for kids

I'm a massive advocate of 'casting a vote for the world you want' when spending my money, but it took me a long time to cotton on to the power of any money I might have sat in savings to create a better world.

Many of us will want to set up an ISA or a savings account for our children (or grandparents might want to), and the very last thing we want is to think that those savings might be being used to fund things like fossil fuels, which are actively working against the future that we want for our children.

Fortunately there is now a wide range of 'ethical' or 'positive impact' savings accounts available, which are working as hard as you are to ensure our kids have a safe and secure future. And the other good news is that ethical investments are often now outperforming traditional ones in terms of returns, so your choice of savings account really can have a doubly positive impact on your child's future.

Triodos (www.triodos.co.uk) are an 'ethical bank' with a range of different savings accounts and ISAs, and the Good With Money website (www.good-with-money.com) is a great place to start when you're looking for suggestions of ethical ISAs and accounts.

Feeding your baby

There is already enough guilt around how you may or may not choose to feed your baby, and I am not here to tell you that one way is 'better' than any other.

What I am going to do is share with you some tips for making whichever way you feed your baby a little bit greener. And remind you that yet again, it doesn't have to be one way or the other. Lots of people mix it up. You do you.

BREASTFEEDING

Reusable breast pads

If you're breastfeeding, it's more than likely that you're finding yourself getting through a startling number of breast pads. Have a look around for some reusable ones – there are loads of different options – and just pop them into your normal wash. Don't do what I once did and wash them with the reusable nappies – you WILL get mastitis…

Nipple cream

I remember using Lansinoh (a cream made from the lanolin in sheep's wool) on my poor sore nipples when breastfeeding – not sure if it actually made any difference, but it made me feel like I was doing something that might help. It does however come in difficult to recycle plastic tubes, so if you're looking for something that's kind to the planet as well as your nipples, check out Valley Mist Baby & Nipple Balm (www.valleymist. co.uk) (which doubles as a nappy balm/cream) and is in a glass jar.

Feeding cover/shawl things

When we first start to venture out of the house, the thought of having to get your boobs out in front of total strangers to feed your baby can understandably feel a little daunting. But I promise you, it will soon feel really easy and natural and you'll be able to do it so discreetly that many people won't even notice (I once answered the door to the postie with a baby latched on…). So instead of forking out for a brand new all-singing all-dancing cover, either ask a friend if they've got one you can borrow, or make use of the wonderful all-rounder that is the muslin cloth (you're always bound to have one of these in your changing bag, and it's one less thing to have to carry around).

Breastfeeding clothes

I don't remember buying a huge amount of special breastfeeding clothes. The one thing I found really useful was a couple of breastfeeding vests, simply so I that could hoik up my top, and still have something covering up my post baby belly.

Have a look on eBay or at NCT sales to pick up some secondhand bargains, or if you want to splash out on a couple of new items, Frugi (welovefrugi.com) do some lovely ethically made breastfeeding tops that you'll want to keep wearing long after your baby is weaned.

BOTTLE FEEDING

Bottles and teats

Glass bottles are widely available and can be used as an alternative to plastic ones. Obviously there is a concern with breakages using glass bottles, but one company, Hevea Planet (www.heveaplanet.com), have come up with an ingenious natural rubber spherical cage type thing that goes around their glass bottles. They make it easier for you and your baby to hold, and protect from any breakages if dropped. You can also get stainless steel ones that you can continue to use as your baby grows, by simply swapping the teat for different lids – have a look at Pura (www.purastainless.co.uk). I'm assured that it's fine to use both secondhand bottles and teats as they will be regularly sterilised anyway – just always check carefully for any cracks or splits in the teats.

Sterilising

Steam sterilising is a good option as it doesn't use any chemicals. You can get plug-in electric versions or ones that go in the microwave. Again, see if you can find one secondhand, or borrow one from friends who are in between babies. Don't forget if you're just using the odd bottle here and there, you can save yourself some money, plastic and work-top space by simply boiling the bottles for 10 minutes.

Formula

The most important thing to note here is that you find a formula that suits your baby – if they need a prescription formula, or will only drink a specific one, please don't sweat it. Having said that, here are a few pointers:

- Nestlé (who make SMA) generally gets a bad rap in ethical terms for its 'irresponsible marketing of breast milk substitutes' in the developing world.
- Danone (Aptamil and Cow & Gate) are also on the boycott list from the Baby Milk Action network (www.babymilkaction.org) for similar reasons.

• If we follow the 'reduce' principle of our waste hierarchy (*see* page 20), buying the biggest box/can etc. of formula you can find (once you're sure your baby likes it!) is probably one of the best ways of reducing the impact of packaging. Single-use bottles and cartons are super convenient, but have a greater impact on the planet and your bank balance! If you do plump for the single-use portions when out and about, the plastic bottles are easier to recycle than tetrapacks.

Dummies

This is (yet) another area that seems to generate a huge amount of debate and judgement, which we're totally not going to go into here! In my view, you do whatever you need to do to get your baby to sleep and to help you stay sane. However, before researching this book it never even occurred to me to explore whether there were 'eco-friendly' options for dummies. And it turns out there are! Which is great news, especially when some sources recommend that dummies should be replaced every six to eight weeks for hygiene reasons…

Hevea Planet (www.heveaplanet.com) are a Danish company that make dummies from natural rubber from sustainably managed rubber trees. Being made from natural rubber means that the dummies are theoretically biodegradable and can be composted (although I couldn't find any information as to how long they should take to break down). Hevea Planet have also started a scheme where you can send your old dummies back to them to be upcycled, which sounds like a pretty good plan to me!

Baby clothes

When we think about 'fast fashion' (cheap, mass-produced clothes) we tend to think about our own clothes, but baby garments are not exempt. It can be really tempting to stock up on adorable cheap babygros and outfits, only to find that they've grown out of them before they've even been worn.

Babies generally outgrow seven clothing sizes in their first two years, and a third of parents have thrown away perfectly wearable outgrown baby clothes because they didn't know what else to do with them.

Remember to refer back to the buyerarchy of needs (*see* page 13) when you're looking for clothes for your new precious bundle – here are a few extra options:

BABY CLOTHES RENTAL

Renting clothes rather than buying means that one set of clothes can be used by multiple babies. It saves you the time of trawling round the charity shops, and you still get to do your bit for the planet.

- Check out Bundlee (www.bundlee.co.uk) for a monthly subscription service where you receive 15 items of ethically made and super stylish baby clothes. The subscription includes insurance against stains and wear and tear, so you can use them worry-free, and then get sent your next bundle as your baby grows!
- Belles and Babes (www.bellesandbabes.co.uk/baby) works in a very similar way, providing you with a bundle of 18 high-quality items worth £300–400 for just £35 per month.
- Graceful Changes (www.gracefulchanges.co) is a family-run business based in Edinburgh established to reduce waste and save parents time and money, delivering 15 items of organic, quality baby clothes for a monthly fee.

SECONDHAND

Buying secondhand is undoubtedly cheaper and better for the planet, but maybe you just don't have the time or headspace to trudge round the charity shops, or to scour eBay or endless Facebook groups.

- Pure Bundle (www.purebundle.co.uk) is a great idea. Select from 'capsule wardrobes', of varying genders and sizes, all from sustainable quality brands and carefully curated to enable mixing and matching (I totally wish someone would create this service for grown-ups). When they're outgrown, you have the option to sell them back to be used again.
- Another option is Loopster (www.loopster.co.uk) – a website listing secondhand baby and kids clothes that have all been carefully checked to ensure they're good quality.

BUYING NEW

If you're looking to buy new clothes for your baby, or want somewhere to point eager grandparents, these are some great sustainable brands:

- **FRUGI (WWW.WELOVEFRUGI.COM)**
  Gorgeous organic vests and babygros, as well as gro-bags and cot sheets, all ethically made.

- **KITE (WWW.KITE-CLOTHING.CO.UK)**
  These beautiful clothes are made in Dorset in the UK from sustainable materials, with all the elements in the supply chain – ranging from the cotton grower to the embroiderers – inspected to ensure that they meet comprehensive organic and ethical standards.

- **LITTLE GREEN RADICALS (WWW.LITTLEGREENRADICALS.CO.UK)**
  Another British brand supplying organic and fairtrade baby clothes, all designed to adjust and grow with your child, and to be passed on from one child to the next.

5 QUICK WINS WITH A NEW BABY

1 Look online to see if you have a nappy library near you and take a visit to have a chat. Speaking to a 'real person' about reusable nappies makes it feel much less daunting (I promise!).

2 Have a try with reusable wipes, even if it's just at home to start with.

3 Wash at 30°C with an eco-friendly washing powder or liquid – you will suddenly find you are doing a LOT of washing!

4 Could you commit to finding a certain percentage of baby clothes secondhand? What feels do-able?

5 If you can, grant yourself a cuppa and sit down when the baby sleeps (easier with first babies than subsequent ones, so make the most of it!). Nothing eco about this one at all, but who needs a bigger to-do list with a new baby?

Over to you

What will you try? Remember that with a new baby, you're on a steep learning curve. Be gentle with yourself, but if you did want to try out some changes, what would they be?

Brainstorm just one or two things you could try out and list them below (I normally say three to four things, but in the new baby stage, if you manage to have a shower some days that can be an achievement, so let's be gentle with our ambitions and any additional pressure we're putting on ourselves).

Action	Timeframe
1.	
2.	
3.	
4.	

Resources

- NATIONAL CHILDBIRTH TRUST (WWW.NCT.ORG.UK)
  A great point of contact for local nappy libraries and 'nearly new' sales.

- THE NAPPY LADY (WWW.THENAPPYLADY.CO.UK)
  A great website packed with information and resources for all things reusable nappies.

- UK NAPPY NETWORK (WWW.UKNAPPYNETWORK.ORG)
  Find your nearest nappy library.

- *THE JOY OF REUSABLE NAPPIES*; LAURA TWEEDALE, BOW BIRD PRESS, 2020
  This book answers the 10 biggest questions parents ask when they start to think about reusable nappies, in a supportive and gently encouraging way.

CHAPTER

4

Bigger babies

'The days are long but the years are short.'

Gretchen Rubin, author of
The Happiness Project

This is such an apt quote for those early months (years?) of parenthood. Time may well feel like it has slowed down, especially during those interminable night feeds, or on those days when they just point blank refuse to have a nap. But before you know it, you'll no longer be the proud parent of a newborn, you'll feel lost if you leave the house without your massive changing bag, and you'll be starting to think about weaning…

Weaning

We opted for baby-led weaning with both of ours, not because of any deep-seated desire to avoid pouches and bottles of baby food (I had yet to have my 'sustainable(ish)' epiphany), but more out of sheer laziness. I just couldn't face the thought of gleefully (or even grumpily) boiling up fruit and veg and pureeing them into all kinds of revolting looking concoctions, at the same time as having to feed ourselves (and then a toddler second time around).

Whether you choose to do baby-led weaning, or to go down the puree route, or a mash-up of the two, is absolutely your choice to make, with no judgement whatsoever. Here are some ideas for greener weaning.

POUCHES

While pouches of pre-prepared food might be a godsend in terms of ease and convenience, they aren't such great news for the planet. Because they're made up of mixed materials (plastic and aluminium) they're difficult to recycle, meaning that the vast majority end up in landfill. Which as we know by now is Not Good. But fear not, there are sustainable(ish) options out there, meaning you can still enjoy the convenience of pouches without the guilt.

TERRACYCLE SCHEMES

Baby food brand Ella's Kitchen have partnered with recycling company Terracycle to create a recycling scheme for any brand of baby food pouches. You can check on the Terracycle website to see if you have a drop-off point near you (www.terracycle.com/en-GB/brigades/ellacycle). You need to 'make sure all excess product has been removed' (it's good practice to give them a rinse and then pop the caps back on) and drop them at your nearest drop-off point. They are collected and shredded, and the resultant pellets of material are then used to create new recycled products and packaging.

LITTLE FREDDIE'S RECYCLING SCHEME WITH ENVAL

Little Freddie (www.littlefreddie.com) is a British baby food brand that has partnered with 'recycling innovator' Enval. The difference between this scheme and the Terracycle one, is that Enval have developed technology that enables them to separate the pouch's aluminium and plastic layers so that they can be reused, resulting in a 90 per cent reduction in the carbon footprint than other methods for recycling baby food pouches.

You can pick up a special recycling bag for 99p from Sainsburys stores, or online at Ocado, and then simply fill it with any brands of pouches and pop it in the post.

REUSABLE POUCHES

These are now widely available, and if we think back to our wonderful waste hierarchy, reusing is nearly always a better option than recycling! Although they don't have quite the same convenience as the pre-filled pouches, with a little bit of forward planning they can work really well and will save you money as well. You can fill them with homemade smoothies and purees, and then use them as you would a 'normal' pouch. They can be pre-filled and frozen, and when they're empty you can whack them in the dishwasher. They also work really well for yoghurt in lunch boxes for older kids, too. And of course, 'traditional' baby food in small glass bottles that can be recycled or re-used is a great option.

3 reusable pouches

1 Nom-Nom Kids do a great colourful range of pouches, along with snack packs, and have some brilliant recipes and ideas on their blog (www.nomnomkids.co.uk).

2 Squeasy Snacker (www.onco.co.uk/products/squeasy-snacker) – these are silicone bottles with a no-spill insert that can be used for smoothies and yoghurts and also for drinks.

3 Doddle Bags (www.doddlebags.com) are reusable pouches that come with a range of different attachments, so you can have the regular spout thing, or attach a spoon, or even a brush for mess-free(ish) painting once the kids are bigger!

Feeding bits and bobs

HIGH CHAIRS

My main criteria when we were looking for a high chair for our eldest was that it would be easy to clean. So many of them seem to come with soft squidgy plastic coverings that I'm sure make dining a very comfortable experience for the small person, but seem to make cleaning up afterwards a nearly impossible task for the grown-up. And the grubbier and more stained they are, the harder they are to pass on to people once your kids have grown out of them.

3 of the best high chairs

1. We opted for the indestructible Ikea *Antilop* high chair, which was incredibly easy to keep clean and survived two children to be passed on in good condition. It was also relatively transportable as it's lightweight and the legs pop off, so we were able to take it with us on holidays and when visiting grandparents etc.

2. Buying with longevity in mind, another great option from Ikea is their *Langur* model, that starts out as a high chair then grows with your child so that it can be used as a regular chair of varying heights as they get older.

3. If you're not on a tight budget, or you want something to suggest to grandparents to buy, then you can't beat the Stokke Tripp Trapp® chair. It has an extension set to allow you to attach a baby seat, then works as a high chair and then adapts all the way up so that it can be used by adults. They're also incredibly durable and come in a range of gorgeous colours.

BABY PLATES, BOWLS AND CUTLERY

As with most things baby, there is now a bewildering array of different baby bowls, plates, knives, forks and spoons in temptingly lovely designs, any number of different shapes, and all kinds of different materials. My advice here again would be to choose with durability in mind. We were given a really lovely melamine bowl, plate and cup set once for our kids, and I'm not exaggerating when I say that the cup was dropped on its first outing out of the box and smashed into a number of small pieces on our tiled floor.

If you don't mind the odd scratch and a slightly faded pattern, then ask around friends and family to see if they've got anything suitable still hanging around from when their kids were smaller. And keep your eye out in charity shops and at car boot sales as well – if you start looking early, you should hopefully get lucky!

- Try to avoid anything character based – your train-mad child might adore Thomas the Tank Engine when he's two, but maybe not so much when he's five (although to be fair, this is a bad example as the appeal of Thomas tends to be fairly long-lived in my experience).
- Resist the temptation to get anything personalised. Subsequent siblings will undoubtedly point blank refuse to use anything with their older brother or sister's name on it, and it will make it very difficult to pass on once you're no longer using it.
- Buy with 'bounceability' in mind – the reason we don't let our kids run amok with our regular plates is that we're worried they'll drop them and break them. So there's no point buying kids' stuff that will break when dropped (see my point above).
- If you've got a dishwasher (*confession: we have, and I wouldn't be without it, despite the ongoing dispute in the eco world over which is more eco*) make sure it can be chucked in there. There's nothing more annoying than having to wash up the kids' stuff separately.
- Go for gender neutral colours – again this makes using them for any more kids that you might have easier, as well as passing on afterwards.
- For spoons, knives and forks, look out for ones that will still be going strong when your little ones are a bit bigger (but not yet ready for wrestling with a grown-up sized fork). We've got some that have hard plastic handles and metal ends of the knife/fork/spoon and our youngest (now aged nine) still happily uses them.

Bamboo tableware for kids has seen a massive rise in popularity in the rush to move away from plastic. However, the important thing to note here is that plastic in this scenario isn't necessarily a Bad Thing because we're not talking about single-use plastic.

Bamboo is a very eco-friendly material as it grows so quickly and needs relatively little in the way of water and pesticides, however when it's used in things like cups and plates, it needs to be mixed with a melamine (plastic) resin, which a recent study shows can release toxic chemicals including formaldehyde when used for hot drinks.

Another option is actually plastic plates – IKEA do a great colourful range that many reusable party kits have opted to use (*see* page 103). They seem pretty indestructible and will double up as picnic and partyware once the kids are older.

A good old-fashioned choice is enamel plates and bowls that were traditionally used for camping. They won't break if you drop them, they can go in the dishwasher and the whole family can use them. They should even last to become heirlooms and passed on to the grandkids!

BIBS

Oh my goodness, you will need **all** the bibs. And they WILL get destroyed (how does one banana do so much damage?!). First up, avoid white bibs. Why are most baby bibs white when their sole function is to absorb food spills?

Although we had some of the ones that are fabric on top of a thin layer of plastic, in hindsight, with my sustainable(ish) head now on, I would try to avoid these – they will be difficult to recycle due to being mixed materials.

The more rigid bibs with the bucket-y bit at the bottom are a good option if you've got a very messy eater, or a very sloppy dinner, and should last to be passed on to other kids – again, avoid white/pale colours, especially with tomato pasta sauce.

Orange Bibs (www.orangebibs.com) are a Manchester-based company started up by a husband and wife team who found themselves asking the question, 'Why are all baby bibs white when it seems all baby food is orange?' They went on to create orange bibs made from organic cotton, and dyed with vegetable dyes, that have simple straps to tie at the back so that they can grow with your children.

Sleep

COTS

In the blink of an eye your precious bundle that once looked so tiny lying in their Moses basket will soon be waking themselves up bashing against the sides and you'll be looking to move them into a cot.

Cots are pretty robust and the kind of thing you might get handed down if you've got family or friends who've got older kids. Again, have a look for one secondhand – if there's a particular 'on-trend' brand you're seeking (is there such a thing as an 'on trend' cot? I'm too off-trend to know) then eBay can be a good place to look; just remember to tick the 'used' box when you narrow down your search.

If you're looking for new, then again, repeat after me, buy with longevity in mind.

I've just discovered these cots from Boori (www.boori.com/uk) that start as a cot, convert into a toddler bed, and then either a full-sized single bed, or a sofa bed. So you really could have one bed that takes you from just after birth to leaving home (although I'm told most teenagers insist on a double bed nowadays). These tick a LOT of sustainable(ish) boxes – made from sustainably sourced wood, painted with eco-paints, built to last – although the biggest drawback I can see is that they're manufactured in Australia, so obviously come with a fairly hefty carbon footprint shipping them over here. However, bear in mind that if your regular cot is made in China, that also comes with a similar transport footprint.

Stokke (www.stokke.com) also do a cot that will take your child from birth to 10 years with a range of separately sold extension sets with their trademark Scandi aesthetic.

If you've just got a standard cot, remember to try and pass it on when your kids outgrow it, and failing that, get lost down the Pinterest rabbit hole of 'cot upcycles' and turn it into a desk, bookshelf, garden furniture or something else!

MATTRESSES

Moses basket and cot mattresses are one of the few things that aren't advised to be sought secondhand (*see* page 17), even as your child grows. When you're looking for a new mattress, look out for 'eco-friendly' ones. You can get mattresses made entirely from natural fabrics like organic cotton and pure wool, or alternatively mattresses made from recycled plastic bottles.

Mattresses can be difficult to recycle and have a very low recycling rate (around 13 per cent), meaning many are consigned to landfill (at best) or fly-tipped (at worst). When you do need to get rid of your cot mattress, it's really worth going the extra mile to see if you can ensure it's actually recycled rather than left to rot in landfill. If you're buying a new mattress for a toddler or single bed, ask the company you're buying from if they offer a service whereby they will collect the old one and recycle it for you, harvesting as many materials as possible for reuse – many will do this (but will charge). Collect Your Old Bed (www.collectyouroldbed.com) is a company that provides a nationwide collection service for mattresses and guarantee to leave nothing to waste.

First steps

I once heard a saying that we spend the first few years of our child's life desperate for them to walk and talk, only to spend the next 15 years telling them to sit down and shut up! A little bit harsh maybe, but I vividly remember how keen we were for number one to walk (not so much number two, I think most parents want subsequent children to stay put for as long as possible!). And those first wobbly steps will always be really precious moments. But as soon as they're walking it feels necessary to start parting with what feels like a disproportionately large sum of money for very small pairs of shoes that will be very quickly outgrown. (A pattern that will continue pretty much until they leave home, with larger and larger pairs of shoes.)

It can feel like there's a lot of pressure on us to indulge in that rite of passage that is baby's first pair of shoes, and unsurprisingly manufacturers have cottoned onto this with Clarks now listing 'crawler shoes' on their website. Clearly I'm not a podiatrist, but from what I've read by people who are, before children can walk the only function of shoes is to keep their feet warm or cool, and that wearing shoes too early can actually do more harm than good. So until your little one is confidently walking on their own outside, keep your money in your purse and let them run barefoot.

Once they are walking with ease (and very likely at this point refusing to go into the buggy, meaning any journey takes about 500 times longer than it should) that's the time to look for that milestone first pair. Babies' feet are very soft and squishy, and not just on the outside but on the inside too, as the bones in their feet won't have 'ossified' (turned to bone) fully. Meaning that it's quite easy for poorly fitting shoes, or shoes not specifically designed for delicate feet, to cause damage.

Walking barefoot is also really important for the normal development of baby's feet as well as helping their feet to feedback to their brains to help balance and co-ordination improve. According to paediatric podiatrist Tracy Byrne the important things to look out for are flexible soles, wide toe boxes without tapering, and natural lightweight materials. It's commonly thought that we should avoid secondhand kids' shoes as they will have moulded to the shape of another child's feet, but given how quickly babies' feet grow and how little they wear them, as long as you're confident the fit is OK and they are a good quality shoe (with all the attributes above) you could easily pick up some barely worn first shoes for a fraction of the new price, saving the shoes from landfill, and your pocket from a little bit of 'shoe strain'.

Vivo Barefoot (www.vivobarefoot.com) are a shoe brand that aims to mimic the benefits of barefoot walking whilst providing feet with protection from the terrain. Their shoes start from a child's size four, and their toddler range is made from recycled plastic, meaning a big thumbs up from the planet as well.

First aid kit

Pre-kids, you probably never gave much thought to having a first aid kit, other than maybe a packet of plasters kicking around in case you got a blister. However, once you have kids, you will probably find that your medicine cabinet expands a little. Here are a few eco-friendly options.

THERMOMETER

We had never owned a thermometer and didn't even think about the fact that we might need one, until we did need one. In the middle of the night, with a screaming baby who wouldn't settle, wondering if they might have a temperature. Needless to say we went out and bought one the very next day. We've got a digital ear thermometer, and I'm sure it's highly frowned upon, but we don't bother with the little disposable plastic caps that you're supposed to use with them.

PLASTERS

Our youngest went through a phase of LOVING plasters – the slightest bang or bump needed a plaster, regardless of whether there was even a drop of blood. Now obviously I should have just stood my ground and refused, but when you're knackered and just need to move on from the tears and tantrums resulting from said 'trauma', it was often easiest to just stick on a bloody plaster. However, most plasters are plastic-based, and I would always feel slightly guilty about the extra plastic that was headed for the bin just because I needed the wailing to stop.

Enter PATCH plasters (www.patchstrips.eu) – a bamboo plaster made without plastic and chemicals.

CALPOL AND NUROFEN

Don't panic, I'm not going to suggest you try and make do without these parenting essentials! However, if you can avoid the sachets, please do. I once bought some to keep in the changing bag, and then found them two years later, obviously out of date and I'd never needed to use them. My big bugbear with children's medicine bottles is the apparent need to provide a new syringe with every bottle, meaning that households with young children have a drawer somewhere overflowing with the things. Apparently it's not just me who finds this infuriating, as there are petitions on petition platforms calling for an end to this. I don't have any smart ideas to work around this, other than maybe signing one of the petitions. The syringes can be re-purposed into bath toys, used for painting, and failing all else, should be recyclable with the 'hard plastics' at your recycling centre.

SUN CREAM

Sun creams can be laden with chemicals that not only have potentially adverse effects on us, but can also damage marine life if we use them and then swim in the sea. Look for organic and cruelty-free versions, like Odylique (www.odylique.co.uk) and Green People (www.greenpeople.co.uk) who do an easy to apply formula especially for kids.

If you're looking for a plastic-free sun cream, there is a UK brand called Shade (www.shadecream.com) that comes in a metal tin, however it needs to be re-applied every 15–20 minutes, which might make it less appealing given how traumatic it seems to be to put sun cream on kids…

Other stuff

Bear in mind that when babies are this age they are growing very quickly, both size wise and developmentally. What feels like a 'must have' piece of kit will very soon be languishing gathering dust and taking up valuable space. Things like Bumbo seats (we bought one, and I think our eldest sat in it happily for approximately eight minutes and our youngest point blank refused) and Jumperoos (huge noisy things that you sit your baby in and they can then bounce around bashing the flashing lights and generally making a lot of noise) can be a godsend providing you with precious minutes of time to go to the loo unencumbered by a grizzling baby, but they can be expensive and resource intensive, especially when viewed from a cost per use basis.

Always ask friends and family to see if they've got one – we borrowed a Jumperoo from a friend and I was very glad to be able to hand it back again after just a couple of months!

Keep your eye out at NCT and 'nearly new' sales – they're the kind of thing that everyone buys thinking they need to have one, and then very quickly either wishes they hadn't (they're irritatingly noisy) or the baby doesn't like it.

Check out Whirli (www.whirli.com) on page 97 – a toy subscription site that allows you to borrow items. They have toys on there suitable from birth up to about aged eight years, including big items like Jumperoos, bouncy rocking chairs, and baby gyms. I wish it had been around when ours were little!

5 QUICK WINS WITH BIGGER BABIES

1. Invest in a cot that can grow with your baby and will last for years.

2. If you're using pouches, look to find your nearest Terracycle collection point, or get a returns envelope to take part in the Little Freddie recycling scheme.

3. Try out reusable pouches, even if it's just some of the time. There's also the option of simply decanting your homemade purees into good old Tupperware pots when you're out and about.

4. Once your baby has outgrown their Moses basket, investigate getting the mattress recycled (or see if you can get inventive and find a new use for it – it would make a great pet bed!).

5. Look out for dark coloured bibs!

Over to you

What will you try? Brainstorm three to four things you could try out and list them below:

Action	Timeframe
1.	
2.	
3.	
4.	

Resources

- *THE BABY-LED WEANING COOKBOOK;* JILL RAPLEY AND TRACEY MURKETT, VERMILION, 2010

  Whichever route you decide on for weaning, it's always great to have some recipes up your sleeve that the whole family can eat, along with easy snacks.

- TERRACYCLE BABY FOOD POUCHES COLLECTION POINTS (WWW. TERRACYCLE.COM/EN-GB/BRIGADE_GROUPS/KIDSFOODPOUCH-UK)

  Search on the website for collection points near you.

- LITTLE FREDDIE RECYCLABLE POUCHES (WWW.LITTLEFREDDIE.COM/ PAGES/PLANET)

  More detail can be found on this website about the recycling scheme between Little Freddie and Enval.

Toddlers and pre-schoolers

As your bundle of joy continues to grow and explore, so will your need to find ways to keep them entertained, and very quickly your house might take on the look of the John Lewis toy department when it's been ram-raided by a group of toddlers.

Toys

Apparently the average child in the UK receives around £350 worth of toys a year. When I first discovered this statistic I was very sceptical. I was also slightly smug thinking that we were way off this figure given that we buy most of the kids' toys secondhand, and 'how ridiculous that people spend that much on toys'. But then I stopped for a minute and thought about Christmas, and birthdays, and gifts from relatives, and saw how it could quickly add up. And we also all know that most of these new toys have a novelty value for a day or two (if we're lucky) and are then quickly discarded to act as trip hazards and dust collection points. Here are some ideas for how to limit the influx.

HOW TO LIMIT THE NUMBER OF TOYS IN YOUR HOME

Rotate the toys

I've never been organised enough to give this a go, but I'm reliably informed by those who are winning at parenting that this works quite well. Basically, you squirrel away some toys so they're no longer being played with, and as boredom starts to set in with what's on offer, swap them in, and spirit some of the discarded toys away.

Rent toys

Whirli (www.whirli.com) is a toy subscription site that for a monthly fee allows your kids to choose the toys they want, play with them until they're bored, and then return them to choose a whole new set. The toys are all thoroughly inspected, cleaned and disinfected when they arrive back at Whirli HQ, and if your child falls in love with a toy and doesn't want to send it back, it's not a problem. They are also very accepting of the fact that 'accidents happen'…

NB A Whirli subscription is a brilliant suggestion for over-zealous grandparents, as they get to feel like they are constantly 'buying' new toys for the kids, and you can send back any you don't like/that they get bored of quickly, to exchange for something less noisy/irritating.

Have a toy swap party

Get together with your playgroup, school, or with friends who have kids of similar ages to yours, and have a toy swap party. We did a 'give and take' at school and it worked really well. However, with younger kids you might want to do it without them there, otherwise there **will** be wails as they decide that the toys you selected to swap are their favourite toys ever and can't possibly be parted with, despite the fact that you found them shoved under the bed and covered in dust.

Buy secondhand

Charity shops are awash with toys and books, as are NCT sales, and you can pick up some absolute bargains. eBay can also be good if you're looking for specific things like Lego sets – our boys are now quite accepting of the fact that Lego doesn't always come in a sealed cardboard box.

Operate a 'one in, one out' policy

We like a mooch around the charity shops, and the kids quickly cottoned on to the idea that I was far more amenable to buying them toys in there, than from the toy shop. However, just because they're mostly secondhand toys, doesn't mean there aren't still *too many* toys. So I started to instigate a one in, one out rule – if they saw something they wanted, they had to tell me what thing they would get rid of (donate to the charity shop) to create the space. I'd love to say it works perfectly, but they seem to have also cottoned on to the fact that I usually forget to get them to seek out the toy that they are willing to sacrifice by the time we get home (do as I say, not as I do!).

TOY RECYCLING

If your kids have abandoned some of their toys, and moved on to newer, more exciting ones, as long as the toy is still in usable condition please do pass it on for others to enjoy. This can be done by passing them on to younger friends and relations, or donating to a local charity shop. Some hospitals will take toy donations for their children's wards or waiting areas (do check first), and some women's refuges will also gladly rehome toys (again, please do check first).

But there will always be those toys that are beyond repair and not fit to be passed on – what then? In 2020, Hasbro linked up with recycling firm Terracycle to start a toy recycling scheme. Any Hasbro brand toy (Hasbro toys include Nerf, Transformers, Ben and Holly and more), including board games, dolls, action figures and plush toys, can be dropped off at one of the designated collection points and will then be recycled. Check out www.terracycle.com/en-GB/brigades/hasbro-uk for more info.

TOP TIPS FOR PESTER POWER

This is the age when 'pester power' starts to kick in. Couple that with 'toddler tantrums' and you can be in for a real treat (usually slap bang in the middle of the supermarket with everyone staring at you).

I naively thought that spending a year buying nothing new at a young age would mean that our kids would be somehow magically immune to the lure of clever marketing and bright shiny new things. Ha! Seared into my memory is the meltdown in the magazine aisle of the supermarket that resulted from the refusal to give in to demands for a kids' magazine encrusted with 'instant landfill' (the plastic tat that apparently it's compulsory to festoon kids' magazines with). Here are my totally non-expert parenting strategies for attempting to deal with pester power without meltdowns (from kids or grown-ups):

- **SET YOUR BOUNDARIES AND TRY AND STICK TO THEM**
  If you don't want the kids to have magazines covered in plastic crap, avoid the magazine aisle! And maybe create some 'rules', like they can only have one on long car journeys, or if you're going on holiday, or at the end of term as a special treat.

- **TRY EXPLAINING**
  During the infamous magazine aisle tantrum I remember trying to explain to our incoherent three-year-old that he couldn't have the magazine he so desperately wanted because of all the plastic tat. Obviously at the time the only effect that had was to increase the volume of the wailing and I assumed it had fallen on deaf ears. However, we had another chat about it when he was calmer and the next time they were allowed to choose a magazine he surprised me by proudly explaining to me that he was choosing one with less plastic on the front to help the animals.

- **PLAY FOR TIME**
  Even though every time it is against my better judgement, I still somehow manage to get whinged into letting the kids go into the toy shop in the nearby town. And even though every time I say as we enter, 'You know we're not buying anything don't you?' there are still the inevitable pleas for all the shiny new toys. One tactic that seems to work is to take a picture on my phone and tell them that if they still remember it and want it in a week's time we can have a think about getting it. Ninety-nine per cent of the time they forget.
  NB This tactic also works for us as grown-ups – if you're window shopping and see something you really want, snap a pic, and if you still remember it and want it in a week's time you can have a look on eBay as a first step.

A SPECIAL WORD ON THE PLASTIC TAT THAT COMES WITH KIDS' MAGAZINES

I understand entirely why they do it – it's the plastic toys that lure most kids into wanting a magazine, not the fact that they can learn their phonics or read a fun story or that there are educational games inside. But it's estimated that over 150 million toys are given away on the front of all UK kids' magazine per year, equating to around 3000 tonnes of plastic. The vast majority of this will end up in landfill literally within minutes of being unpacked (it usually breaks), will very rarely survive to be passed on to other children, and is difficult to recycle.

I try very hard not to take the kids food shopping with me, and this is easier now they're both at school and I work from home, but there are times when it can't be avoided. The supermarket we frequent happens to be right next to a charity shop, so my tactic is to promise them they can have a look in the charity shop for a book or comic annual after we've done the shopping (but only if they're good!).

5 KIDS' MAGAZINES THAT COME WITHOUT PLASTIC

1 The *Beano*
   Yep, it's still going strong, and my kids both absolutely love it. My auntie buys them a subscription for Christmas and they anxiously wait for it to arrive in the post each week.
2 *Dot* magazine (www.anorakmagazine.com)
   This is a quarterly magazine for creative kids aimed at boys and girls under five. It's printed on recycled paper and is ad-free.
3 *Whizz Pop Bang* (www.whizzpopbang.com)
   This is a monthly science magazine that is jam-packed with science facts and experiments aimed at kids aged 6–12 years.
4 *Anorak* magazine (www.anorakmagazine.com)
   This interactive kids' magazine has loads of fun stories, drawings and activities 'to keep even the most energetic boys and girls happily engaged'. And as an added bonus it follows the National Curriculum so you can sneak in a bit of school work.
5 *Nat Geo Kids* (www.natgeokids.com)
   Although in the shops this still tends to come with a free gift (they are at least slightly better quality and tend to be things like notepads and rubbers etc.) the subscription version comes gift-free!

Clearly, however, none of these options has any of the allure of the tat-encrusted mags cleverly displayed at kiddy-eye-height in the supermarket, and as we all know it's that 'in the moment' desire that they really want their fix of and not the magazine. But we can try.

Parties and party bags

While we're on the subject of plastic tat, we might as well dive on in and tackle party bags. But before we get there, let's take a look at birthday parties in general as they seem to have morphed from a couple of games of musical chairs and a cake into something a whole lot more elaborate in the gap between my own childhood parties and the ones my kids now seem to expect. Whole class parties are popular, especially in the early years at school (I know this is the toddlers and pre-school chapter, but there's a bit of overlap!) and with them they bring a whole lot of waste – from single-use paper plates and cups, through to balloons and metres and metres of wrapping paper. And that's before we even look at the party bags.

Lots of the general info about baby shower parties (*see* page 46) will apply here, but here's some extra ideas for kids' parties.

INVITES

E-invites (or a quick WhatsApp message) cut down on paper but you may find that they don't quite cut the mustard with an excited four-year-old desperate to hand out their invites to their friends. If you're feeling really keen you can get them to make their own using recycled card (Eco craft – www.eco-craft.co.uk is a really useful site for recycled card blanks and envelopes), but if they desperately want Elsa or Patch from Paw Patrol on their invitations, honestly, don't sweat it.

DECORATIONS
See page 47.

PARTY GAMES
Knock yourself out on Pinterest looking for inventive games that fit your 'theme', but when it comes to prizes, avoid the plastic tat and small plastic bags of sweets and go with some of the suggestions for party bag gifts (*see* page 107).

'Pass the parcel' deserves a special mention, not only for the soul crushing necessity to wrap eleventy billion layers and the time that that takes (usually very late at night the day before the party) but for the volume of paper and Sellotape that it uses up. Some clever souls have come up with the idea of a reusable pass the parcel kit, made of a series of sequentially smaller and smaller fabric bags, ending up with a wooden 'medal' for the winner. Such a genius idea, and before you worry about your lack of sewing skills and the fact that making one of those sounds even more hard work than wrapping with paper, fear not. Many of the reusable party kit suppliers (*see* page 103) also rent these out for a small charge, so you don't even have to find anywhere for it to live in between parties – you simply send it back once you're done.

TABLEWARE
For whole class parties it can feel like the easiest solution is to simply stock up at the supermarket on paper plates, cups and a couple of disposable tablecloths, and simply sling them all into a black bag at the end of the party along with the half-eaten sandwiches and the empty crisp packets. But wait a minute. A whole class party can generate around 100 single-use items headed for landfill – all of which will be sat there rotting long after the birthday boy or girl is all grown up. And while one bin bag of rubbish per party might not seem such a big deal if we're only talking about a couple of parties per year for our own kids, try multiplying that by the number of kids in your child's class. And then the number of

classes in the school. And the number of schools in your town. And it's easy to see very quickly how 'just one bin bag' actually equates to a huge volume of rubbish that could easily be prevented.

Enter the reusable party kit. These have really taken off in the last couple of years and at the time of writing (June 2020) The Party Kit Network (www.partykitnetwork.uk) has nearly 400 kits listed all around the UK. It's such a beautifully simple idea (which is probably why it's caught on so quickly) – one person buys a set of reusable party plates, bowls and cups, and then rents them out to local people having a party. Lots of them also have reusable tablecloths, bunting and decorations, and even the reusable pass the parcel bags (*see* previous page). And if the thought of having to wash it all up is putting you off, many of them offer a washing-up service for a small additional charge.

So for the same cost as single-use items you can have bright, colourful and robust partyware that's helping to save the planet. Three cheers for that!

PRESENTS

A whole class party generates a whole class' worth of presents, which can see the birthday boy or girl overwhelmed with up to 30 gifts on top of the ones they also receive from family. For any child, that's a LOT of presents. For any parent, that's a LOT of room to have to find for it all to live. And for the planet, that's an awful lot of 'stuff' – all of which has used up precious resources and a whole lot of carbon in its manufacture and transport. Not to mention that there's a good chance a lot of it will be plastic.

Receiving presents

Here are some ideas to avoid the influx of presents:

● TRY ASKING FOR 'NO PRESENTS PLEASE'

> *Confession: I once tried asking my then six-year-old if he'd be up for doing this and he looked at me like I was mad. I haven't tried asking him again…*

This option also runs the risk that people will ignore your plea because many of us feel guilty turning up to a party empty-handed.

- **HAVE A 'FIVER' PARTY**

  If there's a bigger item that the birthday girl or boy really wants, like a scooter or a bike, ask everyone to contribute towards it. It can feel a bit uncomfortable, and even somehow a little bit rude, but believe me, most parents will heave a sigh of relief at not having to do the inevitable last-minute dash to the supermarket when they've forgotten to get a gift, desperately trying to pick out something for less than a tenner that your little darling might actually like and not already have.

- **SUGGEST RE-GIFTING**

  Ask the party guests to gift a toy or book of their own that they've really enjoyed playing with or think that your child will enjoy.

I think in order to make any of these ideas actually work, and to not be left with a six-year-old who feels slightly deflated and is maybe wondering why no-one in her class has bought her a present, you need to really have buy-in from the birthday boy or girl. Persuading them that the party itself is celebration enough, without needing all the additional presents, is a tall ask, and as I say, we've not managed it in our house…

TOP TIPS FOR PRESENTS FROM RELATIVES

God this is **such** a tricky one to deal with. And I'm afraid I don't have a nice neat fail-safe solution for you. When my mum was alive she loved to buy gifts for the kids – at birthdays and Christmas she would go mad, but she would also very rarely come to visit empty-handed, and without something fun for the kids and some clothes.

I totally understand that it comes from a place of love, and in our society, we very often see giving presents as a way of expressing that love. And let's be honest, who doesn't love a gift? The problem comes when our kids, and our homes, and our planet, become overwhelmed with the sheer volume of toys, clothes and other bits and bobs. It all comes from somewhere, and it all has to end up somewhere. Sadly, often the charity shop (best case) or landfill (worst case).

So how do we have those tricky conversations with well-meaning grandparents and relatives who would really struggle with requests to not give anything, or just to give something small? Here are some ideas (with varying degrees of subtlety!) that other people have tried:

- **RUTH**

    'We ask my parents to gift our old toys and books to our kids, or find a book/toy they loved as a child or playing with us and read/play them with the kids to "play it forward". They love it as it's nostalgic and I love it because it usually ends up being pre-loved (win-win situation).'

- **NICKY**

    'What I do now is get the presents and let them donate to the cost, and they are happy with that, with a few little extras here and there, which is what everyone enjoys.'

- **LINDA**

    'Ask for specifics. Clothes, magazine or monthly subscription, annual pass, or money towards something specific if it's out of budget. Our six-year-old loved the WWF adoption pack as you get a cuddly toy, poster, info booklet etc. and updates throughout the year.'

- **SARAH**

    'I took a picture of my boy's toys boxed up when we moved and sent it to family members to show just how many toys he had. I then requested specific things. For Christmas this year, I am going to ask for money towards a Whirli subscription. For my eldest's birthday, he got a Mud and Bloom box (a gardening and nature craft subscription box). I make sure I share pictures of him doing it each month to reinforce how amazing it is. I have also told grandparents that he gets very sad when cheap toys break, so it is better to have nothing. A combination of these works to a degree.'

- **CLAIRE**

    'Tell them anything they buy stays at their house for the grandchildren to play with. I'm sure they'll then realise they don't want a house full of crap.'

Giving presents

I have to confess I still find this a really tricky area and when we were spending our year buying nothing new, it was a particular challenge. I made all kinds of homemade gifts like homemade beanbags, cushions, and hair slide tidies, but since then, although my desire to not gift unwanted plastic tat hasn't diminished, my enthusiasm for sewing handmade gifts has. I now have two 'go-tos' both of which can be rustled up on the morning of the party in the very likely scenario that I have forgotten all about it.

- **SHORTBREAD NUMBER BISCUITS**

  If I've got a bit of time I'll rustle up a batch of shortbread dough and use my set of cookie number cutters to cut out some of the birthday boy or girl's age e.g. 4s for a four-year-old. These then get sprinkled liberally with sugar and packaged up in a clean jam jar with a bit of ribbon or colourful twine tied around it.

- **GIANT CHOCOLATE BUTTONS**

  My absolute favourite as they are super quick and always a hit with the kids. Take a 100g bar of chocolate (bonus points if you can find one that's fairtrade and wrapped in paper/cardboard), melt it and then use a teaspoon to dollop out blobs of melted chocolate onto a lined baking tray and smoosh them (technical term) out into giant button shapes. Douse with sprinkles if you happen to have some and leave to set, before packaging up in a jam jar as above.

Obviously you need to check with parents about any allergies etc. if you're going to do either of these. Failing that, a book or book token is generally a pretty safe fall back. (I try to avoid Amazon and gifting Amazon vouchers as I think it's fair to say I'm not their biggest fan in terms of their ethics and sustainability.)

PARTY FOOD

I think we always tend to go a little overboard with kids' food at parties, forgetting that the kids are way too hyper to really sit down and eat much. This tends to lead to lots of food waste, which is, as we now know, a Bad Thing (*see* page 24). One of the best kids' parties I ever went to with ours (food wise) simply had hot dogs, and then massive bowls of strawberries and blueberries for pudding. The kids all wolfed it down, there was very little left over, AND they had all eaten some fruit. At a party!

So keep it simple, and don't over-cater. If possible, buy the biggest bags of crisps etc. that you can, and dole them out into bowls, rather than have lots of individual packets of crisps and biscuits.

Party bags

It's apparently no longer enough to send all the kids home with a piece of cake wrapped in a napkin. Party bags have become more and more elaborate and not only can they end up costing an arm and a leg, they have a tendency towards plastic tat as well.

Needless to say though, kids LOVE them. My youngest once said, 'The whole point of a party is the party bags!' It appears that there is nothing quite like the excitement of diving into a party bag the minute you exit the party to start stuffing your face with (more) sweets and blowing the irritating plastic whistle all the way home.

One option is obviously to take a stand and simply not do them. And if I was braver I would love to do this. But as I mentioned above, our youngest simply refuses to entertain not having party bags. So I've had to get a little bit inventive with our party bags to avoid buying and giving out 'instant landfill'. Here are some ideas for plastic-free(ish) party bags:

The bags themselves

- **GOOD OLD PAPER BAGS ARE A GREAT OPTION**
  You can buy recycled paper ones online from Eco-Craft (www.eco-craft.co.uk). The plain ones are a great idea as you can get the kids to decorate them, which, depending on the kids at the party, will take anything from 30 seconds to 45 minutes. All of which time they are seated and not charging around destroying things.

- **MAKE YOUR OWN PAPER BAGS**
  If you're feeling crafty and have time on your hands (if you do, please can you come and organise my kids' parties for me?) you can make bags from newspapers or magazines – there are some good tutorials online.

- **MAKE YOUR OWN FABRIC BAGS FROM OLD T-SHIRTS OR PILLOWCASES**

  If you're a whizz with the sewing machine, this might be an option for you! T-shirts are super easy to make bags out of – turn them inside out and sew up the bottom of the t-shirt, enlarge the neck hole and chop off the sleeves, turn them the right way round again and you're done! You can even do no-sew versions (search 'no sew t-shirt bags' online) which you could include as a party activity.

Edibles

- Cupcakes, or a piece of cake wrapped in a good old paper napkin, greaseproof paper or foil (avoid clingfilm!).
- Number shaped biscuits – as page 106.
- Chocolate buttons – as page 106.
- Chocolate coins or chocolate eggs – if you remember, at Christmas/Easter time stock up on foil-wrapped Christmas coins and eggs!
- Pick 'n' mix. Who wouldn't love a bag of pick 'n' mix? My kids would have to wrestle me for it. Just don't put the sweets in those plastic cone-shaped bags!

Gifts

- **BOOKS**

  This one will earn you brownie points with the party goer's parents, but the kids may be less enthusiastic! You can often find packs of books where the individual books work out at less than £1 each, so this can be quite an inexpensive option. Either gift on their own, or as part of a party bag if you're feeling very generous.

- **SEEDS**

  A pack of something like sunflower seeds can work well if you have a spring/summer party. Have a competition afterwards to see who can grow the tallest sunflower. Or cress seeds to make a cress head can also be quite fun.

- **COLOURING PENCILS/COLOURING BOOKS**

  Kids can seemingly never have enough colouring pencils and books. Or at least mine can't. You can even get pencils made from actual twigs, which I got once for a forest school party that our eldest had.

- **RECYCLED CRAYONS**

  If you have a stash of crayons that have seen better days, break them all up and melt them in silicone ice cube trays on a very low heat in the oven. We did this once with a Lego brick mould to create Lego-shaped crayons and they were fab.

- **METAL STRAWS**

  If you really want to get little eco-warriors excited about all things plastic-free, then their very own metal straw might go down well!

If you just want someone else to do it for you...

If you don't have the time/energy to spend devoting your life to plastic-free(ish) party bags, then here are some 'done for you' suggestions:

- Plastic-Free Party Bags (www.plasticfreepartybags.com) does what it says on the tin! There's the option of buying pre-filled bags, or just buying the gifts to fill your own.
- Not on the High Street (www.notonthehighstreet.com) has an option to select 'eco-friendly' when you search for party bag fillers.
- Little Otter Party Supplies (www.littleotterpartysupplies.co.uk) has a range of eco-conscious and plastic-free party bag gifts and pre-filled bags.

Sustainable(ish) crafting ideas

Keeping toddlers and pre-schoolers entertained is no mean feat and can feel pretty relentless. Even the least crafty of us will turn to arts and crafts to fill a bit of time on a rainy afternoon and award ourselves some smug parenting points, but sometimes crafting can do more harm than good when it comes to the planet.

GLITTER

Every parent's nightmare but OMG kids love it, don't they?

If the fact that you'll still be finding it sparkling around the house weeks after using it, or turn up at work with a piece stuck to your cheek, isn't enough to put you off, then the revelation that glitter is actually made of teeny tiny pieces of plastic should. It's not just plastic either, it's *micro*plastic, and it's the micro that is especially problematic. You see when our little darlings toddle off to ~~spread glitter all around the~~

sink wash their hands, the glitter travels down the plughole and into our waterways. When it reaches the water treatment plant it's so small that it can pass through the filters, and straight out to sea. It can then be mistaken for food by smaller organisms and enter the food chain.

I had originally intended to say at this point, 'but don't worry, it's not all bad news' and go on to extol the virtues of 'eco-friendly glitter', however a study released by Anglia Ruskin University in October 2020 cast doubt on whether 'eco-glitter' is in fact any more environmentally friendly than it's regular counterparts. If you (or your little ones) really can't face the prospect of glitter-free crafting then my advice would be to check out the Eco Glitter Fun website (www.ecoglitterfun.com) which sells Bioglitter® PURE. This is a plastic-free glitter that has undergone rigorous testing and meets the highest level of independent certification for freshwater biodegradability in the world. Their craft glitter is quite pricey, but maybe you can persuade your kids to take on a 'less is more' approach… If you've got a stash of glitter sat in your craft cupboard that's now making you feel guilty, Eco-Stardust are another eco-friendly glitter company, and they have a 'glitter amnesty' (www.ecostardust.com/pages/non-bioglitter-amnesty). You can send them your pots of glitter (no glitter gels though) and they make it into funky earrings and jewellery (think glitter balls for your ears!) AND give you a 15% discount off their range of eco-glitter.

CRAFT FOAM

Lots of kids' craft packs come with cut-out shapes of craft foam for children to then indiscriminately stick to things. It makes for easy crafting, but as far as I'm aware there's nothing that can be done with them afterwards other than landfill (although obviously we're all keeping every one of our cherub's pieces of artwork for posterity, right?). My advice would be to avoid if at all possible.

STICKY TAPE

Our youngest would frequently be found sitting happily at the kitchen table having raided the recycling bin randomly cutting and taping bits of cardboard and yoghurt pot together, cheerfully rendering them unrecyclable (unless I wanted to spend a good half an hour painstakingly separating it all back out again).

Sellotape recently introduced 'Sellotape Zero' which is plastic-free, and sounds great. However it has to be 'disposed of in industrial composting bins' which very few of us have access to. What we use instead is a paper tape which is plastic-free, and can be composted, or simply left on cardboard boxes so that it's pulped with them and recycled. We get plain brown tape from Eco-Craft (www.eco-craft.co.uk) and found some lovely patterned ones (that stick much better than regular washi tape) from Babipur (www.babipur.co.uk) which work well for gift wrapping etc.

GLUE

Pritt Stick is great for (relatively) mess-free gluing, but it does leave behind the sticky issue (see what I did there) of the plastic tubes to dispose of. PVA might seem like a good idea as you can buy a big bottle and only dollop out a small amount, but the bad news is that it's made from oil.

> Confession: We have a massive 5L bottle of PVA in the cupboard at home that I bought from our local Scrapstore (see page 114) before even thinking about what it's actually made from...

Pentel do a refillable roller glue which is water-based and my kids tell me they use at school, although I couldn't actually find any information on its ingredients anywhere.

One option if you're very keen is to make your own glue – I'm assured it works and is actually pretty easy to do! Anna Broster is an eco-crafting whizz at Le Bus Vert (@lebusvert), and she has kindly shared her recipe:

- Mix one part cornflour to three parts cold water, with a dash of white vinegar or tea tree oil in a pan over a low heat, stirring constantly to avoid lumps, until it thickens.
- While it's still warm, transfer into a glass jar, or this even works well in empty glue sticks.
- The vinegar/oil preserves it, but it does need to be kept in the fridge (make small quantities).
- If the water separates a bit or the mix is too lumpy after a while in the fridge, simply warm it up again in a pan.

PAINT

The good news is that poster paint isn't actually a bad choice when it comes to the planet – it's water-soluble and non-toxic. Things to avoid are acrylic paints (oil-based), and paints mixed with PVA or glitter.

COLOURING PENS AND PENCILS

If you can, colouring pencils are a better choice than felt-tip pens because they're made of wood and can be composted, but I totally accept that that might not be possible (we still have a box of felt-tips, most of which don't actually work…).

ökoNORM are a German company that make eco art supplies for kids and have eco felt-tip pens made with water-based inks. They can be found online at www.babipur.co.uk. Remarkable (www.remarkable. co.uk) do a set of recycled plastic colouring pens, which also look pretty good.

Regardless of what kind of felt-tips you use, remember that they can be recycled when ~~they've been left with the lid off so they've dried up and~~ they no longer work through Terracycle. Most Rymans stores have a collection box, or have a look on the Terracycle website (www.terracycle. com/en-GB/brigades/bic-uk) to find your local collection point.

Another great tip from Anna at Le Bus Vert before you recycle your felt-tips, is to group them all into similar colours and then dunk each colour group into a jar of water and leave for a week. The less water you use, the stronger the colour you get. Cue a great science lesson in diffusion, which can be finished off with experimenting with using the resultant 'ink' that is created, as watercolour paint, or to colour homemade playdough etc. (*see* page 114).

5 TOP TIPS FOR EASY ECO-FRIENDLY CRAFT IDEAS TO DO WITH THE KIDS

In order to reduce your laundry and clothes bill, always make your small person (and indeed your bigger small people) wear aprons for crafting. It doesn't have to be a full-on crafting apron – I remember at primary school we all had to bring in an old grown-up shirt to use.

1 BAKING

In my head, we all gather around the kitchen table with the kids wearing aesthetically pleasing aprons, and have hours of fun baking nutritious goodies, all whilst stealth learning about maths, volume and measuring in a calm and creative environment. Anyone who has attempted baking with small (and even big) children will know that this is very much not the case. However, it's still worth a go (depending on your tolerance for mess, ingestion of raw sugar and baking mix, and lopsided bakes). It has the added benefit of the potential for creating plastic-free(ish) snacks (*see* page 118).

2 JUNK MODELLING

Essentially tip the contents of the recycling bin on the floor and let them loose with some paper tape and glue. Giving them a rough theme (e.g. robots, or spaceships, or buildings) can be helpful to get the creative juices flowing. Loo rolls are always worth saving and it appears the humble loo roll inner knows no bounds when it comes to crafting. They can be used to make bird feeders (coat with peanut butter and roll in bird seed), teeny little gift boxes, and even trains and caterpillars. The only limit is your ~~Pinterest search skills~~ imagination.

3 GROW YOUR OWN

Maybe not strictly a craft, but a great way to while away some time in the garden during the spring and summer, that has the added bonus of teaching kids where their food comes from.

In the same way that you need to let go of any ideas of aesthetically pleasing biscuits when baking, when gardening you need to let go of any idea of planting seeds with any degree of finesse. There will be large amounts of seed dumped in one place, instead of sprinkled lightly. And they will be 'enthusiastically' watered… I know someone who ended up having two separate veg beds – one for the kids, and one for any veg they wanted to have a chance of actually growing.

4 NATURE CRAFT

This essentially means collecting leaves and other things you might find on walks and sticking them onto paper. But you can make it a bit more challenging by seeing if you can find all the colours you need to create a rainbow collage, or make a hedgehog from leaves etc. The advantage with this one is that you get to also fill some time going on a 'nature hunt', which can be helpful if you're having one of those days that never seems to end.

5 HOMEMADE PLAYDOUGH

This is super easy, and keeps really well, so can be dragged out whenever you're at the end of your tether for ideas. I tried a variety of recipes over the years, but they are all much of a muchness – flour, salt, water and a little oil. You can then split your batch up and add food colouring to get different colours, and (eco) glitter if you feel the need for a bit of sparkle. Use cookie cutters for cutting out shapes, and just make sure that you wrap it up and seal it in an airtight container in between uses to stop it drying out.

DID YOU KNOW?

If you're looking for craft supplies for your kids (or indeed yourself) then have a look to see if you have a Scrapstore near you (www.reusefuluk.org./scrapstores-directory). Scrapstores are brilliant projects that take waste from businesses that would otherwise be destined for landfill, and make it available for community groups, schools and individuals to use creatively. Depending on the Scrapstore and the businesses they have donating, you could find bolts of fabric, off-cuts of Burberry leather, cones of yarn and much more. Our local Scrapstore also does kids' craft classes during term-time for pre-schoolers, and during the holidays for older kids, as well as birthday parties.

Food

VEGAN OR VEGGIE MEALS YOUR KIDS WILL ACTUALLY EAT (HOPEFULLY!)

We're all well aware now of the advice to eat less meat and more 'plant-based' meals to help the planet, but when it can sometimes feel like a battle to get our kids to eat anything vaguely healthy, adding in the challenge of rustling up nutritious veggie meals that won't be ~~chucked on the floor~~ rejected can seem like a step too far.

Remember that simple meals like pasta with tomato sauce are 'plant-based', as is beans on toast, or jacket potato and baked beans. So reducing the amount of meat our kids are eating doesn't have to be hard work.

> *Confession: We're not vegan, or even vegetarian. However, we do have at least three or four veggie meals a week, usually without the kids even noticing.*

Rachel Boyett is the author of *Little Veggie Eats* (Vermilion, 2020), and has this advice for parents looking to incorporate more vegetables and plant-based meals:

- Offer a variety of different vegetable-based dishes in separate bowls so that the kids can pick and choose and don't feel overloaded with too many new things on their plate.
- Have dressings and condiments on the side, so that adults can add them for extra flavour, and the children can add as much or as little as they want; consider toppings such as yoghurt, nuts and seeds, pickles and fresh lemon to go on top of things like a veggie curry or chilli to add extra nutrients and different textures.
- Try 'veggie loading' – blend vegetables into other sauces. This isn't really about trying to 'hide' veggies, because I will always be really open and honest with my kids about what's gone into their meals.
- Start using vegetables creatively. Bright coloured veggies, like spinach and beetroot, can add loads of colour to things like pancakes, lollies and smoothies to make them fun and enticing for kids. It also gets them used to eating 'the rainbow' – and especially greens!

- Don't change too much at once; introduce one or two new things at a time. Try to eat seasonally so that your children are getting used to a wide range of vegetables (this is also a great way of reducing costs as in-season vegetables are cheaper).
- Incorporate vegetables into meals they already really enjoy, like pasta, or pies, or making a lentil version of your usual bolognese.

I would add to this as well, to remember the 'ish' – adding extra veg/ lentils to meals can mean that you can easily reduce the amount of meat you're using.

TOP TIPS FOR VEGGIE AND VEGAN DIETS

Lucinda Miller is the clinical lead of NatureDoc (www.naturedoc. co.uk) and runs a team of UK-wide nutritional therapists specialising in woman, child and teen nutrition. She very kindly answered some of my questions about veggie and vegan diets for younger children.

Q Is it safe for under-fives to be vegetarian?
A A healthy vegetarian diet can easily be given to young children, as it usually provides all the nutrients they need to grow and blossom. When following a vegetarian diet it is important that enough iron is given, and this can be found in pulses (especially black beans and kidney beans) as well as green veggies, eggs, oats, peanut butter, molasses and dried apricots. Dairy and eggs can give them the calcium and choline they need, as well making food nice and filling. A vegetarian child will need to top up with a plant-based omega-3 supplement as a veggie diet does not provide enough.

Q Is it safe for under-fives to be vegan?
A Children can thrive on a well-planned vegan diet too, but it's miles harder to provide a well-rounded diet for fully plant-based kids. Hurdles can occur if there are additional

food restrictions present, such as nut allergy or very picky eating. They need to be in the habit of eating plenty of beans, pulses, nut butters, seeds, tofu and vegetables, and you need to work hard on keeping them engaged in eating a broad range of foods and eating enough at each meal. Vegan kids will need topping up with vitamin B12 and a marine algae based omega-3, as a fully plant-based diet cannot provide enough of these for the growing brain. Like vegetarian kids, iron levels need to be monitored too, and you need to include iron-rich foods at least twice a day.

Q What should we be looking out for and making sure we include?
A The best way to nourish a plant-based child is to commit to cooking from scratch as much as possible, as the bought convenience plant-based vegan foods in the shops tend to be highly processed and do not contain that many beneficial nutrients. They may also need to eat more snacks to keep them full up and satiated, and these should always contain some healthy fats and protein. This could be apple slices with peanut butter or hummus with carrot batons.

Q Is it OK for under-fives to have meat replacement products like tofu and Quorn, veggie sausages etc?
A Tofu and tempeh are both excellent sources of calcium and iron as well as protein, so these need to be included in the diet most days alongside pulses, quinoa and nut butters. Many of the Quorn products and specialist veggie meat alternatives contain lots of unnatural ingredients that are devoid of most of the important vitamins and minerals. If the label contains ingredients that you do not recognise as food, then they are unlikely to provide the nutrients your child needs. This is why it is best to cook from scratch so you know your child is getting nutritious food. Every mouthful counts for plant-based kids, especially when they are going through phases of fussy eating or illness.

PLASTIC-FREE(ISH) SNACKS THAT WON'T BREAK YOU WITH A TON OF EXTRA COOKING

It would be going too far to promise you that you can effortlessly rustle up plastic-free snacks for your kids without any extra time in the kitchen, but there are ways to make it easier. Mostly it just needs a little bit of forward planning, and a whole lot of Tupperware pots.

Fruit is your friend

We pretty much never left the house without at least one banana in the changing bag and my husband was always moaning at me when he found manky banana skins that I'd forgotten about wedged into the hood of the buggy. As well as bananas, quickly chop up some apple or pear into slices and whack that in a Tupperware pot to take out with you (if you pack them in tight, they're less likely to go brown. You can also add a small squeeze of lemon juice which helps stop the browning).

Raisins

For ages we would buy the little boxes of raisins and I would inevitably have a pack or two kicking around in my bag, but they come in a plastic bag and can work out really expensive. Eventually I gave up buying them, and just used to grab a handful out of the big bag of raisins in the cupboard that was there for baking, and pop them into a small pot to take out with us. This was much cheaper and I keep the Ziploc bags that they seem to now come in for stashing away cookies etc. in the freezer. Also, if you're lucky enough to have a zero waste shop near you, you should be able to stock up on them plastic-free.

Sandwiches and rolls

If we have nothing else in stock, I will often defrost a roll (we keep ours in the freezer so they don't go mouldy), smear on a scrape of peanut or jam, and pop it into yet another Tupperware pot.

Batch bake

I'm a fan of baking, so it's no hardship to me to spend a Sunday morning pottering around the kitchen baking (especially if my husband is then

~~wrangling with~~ entertaining the kids) but you don't have to be a candidate on *The Great British Bake Off* to make your own snacks. For savoury snacks have a look at things like Nigella Lawson's 'cheesy feet', which are super easy to make, as well as things like oatcakes and mini savoury muffins.

When I've got time to bake I tend to double up batches as I figure it takes pretty much the same amount of time and I've got twice as many snacks, and then I stash stuff in the freezer. My kids have been known to eat frozen biscuits straight from the freezer when I've failed to remember to get anything out in time. I always freeze biscuits once they're cooked (unless they're iced) and will keep a stash of muffins and hot cross buns (minus the crosses – who can be bothered with the faff?) in a bag ready to grab as we head out the door.

FOOD WASTE AND FEEDING YOUNG KIDS

When we're talking about food waste, there are two types. The 'unavoidable', so things like banana skins, veg peelings, egg shells etc. And the 'avoidable', so things like the tub of hummus we opened and then forgot about until it grew a fur coat. And when you've got kids there's a third category – the things they took one bite of and then discarded. You might notice that your food waste seems to rise significantly when you've got kids, and please know that you are not alone. Here are some ideas for using up some of the bits of food your little cherubs have discarded at random around the house.

Banana bread

Obviously. Can't get away without mentioning this. If you've got bananas that are too brown, or that have been peeled and only half-eaten, mash them up into banana bread or muffins. If you don't have time to bake right at that moment, peel them, chop them and whack them in the freezer. You can then defrost them to bake with at your leisure (they will be disgustingly slimy when you defrost them, but will still taste fine!).

Smoothies

Collect up any discarded fruit, wash it, chop it and blend it all into a smoothie. Or you can freeze the chopped fruit until you need it. You can then also decant the smoothie mix into lolly moulds for a refreshing (sneakily healthy) summer treat.

Muffins

Chop up any fruit and add to a basic muffin mix. You can also chuck in those half bowls of porridge or Weetabix that have been left at the breakfast table.

Bread pudding

Save up any crusts, or the end of the loaf that no-one will eat, in a bag in the freezer and then use it to make bread pudding. I also have a bag of half-eaten cheese rolls or bits of toast with peanut butter on that I use to make a savoury version, which is yummy served with baked beans. You can also blitz up bread crusts to make breadcrumbs, which you can freeze and then use to top pasta bakes.

Soup

If you've got any limp veg left at the bottom of the salad drawer that you think the kids will reject, whizz it all up with a stock cube into soup, which you can then also freeze. I've been known to whizz up rejected cauliflower cheese into soup and serve it up the next day when it was eaten without fuss!

Wet weather gear and wellies

I have to say I'm not a great fan of the saying that there's no such thing as bad weather, only the wrong clothing. Personally, I would much rather be warm and dry inside when it's chucking it down, but sometimes you just have to get out of the house. Add to that the fact that for most of the year in the UK, there will nearly always be mud, and if there is mud, kids are going to find it, and the need for wet weather gear and a decent pair of wellies is a must.

ETHICAL WET WEATHER GEAR AND WELLIES

Obviously, the usual advice of hand-me-downs/looking for second-hand etc. applies (hopefully you're getting into the swing of this by now!) but this does involve a degree of forward planning, and keeping your eye out for stuff in advance of the poopy weather/ growth spurts.

I generally fail miserably to plan ahead, so if you're like me, here are a few suggestions for ethical outdoor stuff.

Go Soaky (www.gosoaky.com)

An Amsterdam-based brand that specialise in making high-quality 'outerproofs' that are made to last to be handed from sibling to sibling (or cousin/friend). Their products are PFC- and AZO-free (both toxic chemicals that can cause environmental harm). They only work with certified suppliers, and support penguin projects in the Antarctic.

Muddy Puddles (www.muddypuddles.com)

A British brand 'with a conscience' developing eco-friendly collections made from recycled fabrics and sustainable sourcing and production. They only work with inspected and approved suppliers and support a number of children's charities. They do the whole range of outdoor gear for kids, from raincoats through to waterproof all-in-ones and some bright and funky wellies.

Liewood (www.liewood.com)

Based in Copenhagen, Liewood's ambition is to 'advocate slow living – creating products that will last for generations'. They have a great range of wellies, including ankle length ones (check out the rabbit and panda ones for maximum cuteness), that are made from 100 per cent natural rubber and free from harmful chemicals.

Raising eco-aware kids – part 1

(*See* page 157 for part 2.)

One of the best ways to start engaging our kids in all things eco is to instil in them a love of nature. We only protect what we love, so if we can start to show our children just how amazing our wonderful planet is from a young age, they should hopefully grow up keen to do all they can to help protect it. At this age, keep it really simple – focus on the nature and the world local to you. Talk about the plants and animals you see on your way to the park, and talk about how things change as the seasons change. Feed the birds in your garden, lift up rocks to check out the bugs, spot the bees and butterflies.

MAKE A BIRD FEEDER

This can be as simple as the loo roll inner one suggested on page 113, to a proper full-on wooden bird table. Or anything in between. There are loads of great ideas online for making them out of plastic bottles, or even old teacups and saucers.

Once you're all set up, borrow a book from the library, or download the free 'Seek' app from WWF (World Wildlife Fund) which allows you to take photos of the living things you find, and then identifies them for you and tells you all about them, and get bird spotting! You can also join in with the RSPB's Big Garden Birdwatch in January each year.

MAKE A BUG HOUSE

Again, these can be as simple or as complicated as you want them to be, but the idea is to create an environment for bugs to move into. Collect up bamboo, twigs, old bricks etc. and use them to create a cosy home for all the bugs in your garden. Give them a bit of time to move in and then start exploring and see what you've got.

GO ON A NATURE WALK

This is especially good in spring or autumn, as you can set them the task of 'spotting signs of autumn' etc. You can let them loose with your phone to snap pics, or collect little bits of nature to bring home and create a collage. Another idea is a nature scavenger hunt; make a list of say 10 items they have to find on a walk or a trip to the park – a red leaf, an acorn, a small pebble etc. They don't even have to bring them home, they can simply tick them off a list.

LITTER PICK

I am a massive fan of litter picking! It's such an easy thing to do to make a difference, and a great way with kids to start conversations around plastic and how it might harm wildlife. We got the kids their own litter pickers for Christmas (lucky kids!) and they were delighted with them – we now try and take them with us, along with a bin bag, whenever we go for a walk, and pick up any litter we see along the way. We've even started weighing it when we get back and keeping a tally of the weight for the year. (We got our litter pickers from the 2 Minute Beach Clean website shop – www.beachclean.shop)

Being sustainable(ish) with children with additional needs

Case study

Natasha commented on a Facebook post of mine that she often felt families with disabilities can be invisible in magazines and books, which don't acknowledge their experiences. She very kindly offered to contribute a short piece about her experiences as a parent of a child with additional needs.

Embarking on a journey of a more sustainable lifestyle has not been easy, when adding a child with additional needs into the mix. Many of my own aims, such as cutting back on plastic toys, food and drink in packaging, and waste, have been challenged as I navigate life with a young son with a learning disability and autistic traits.

For him, how items are packaged and look are crucial – it's not simply a case of telling him it's the same drink, but rather it has to be presented in a specific way. Plastic toys are attractive, and he likes the small toys in a Kinder egg. I try to avoid these things, while acknowledging that in his everyday life "reasonable adjustments" have to be made. Likewise in my journey towards increased sustainability.

Along this journey, challenges are faced, including criticisms levelled such as how he is just spoilt or needs to learn and change. But for neurodiverse children, and those with learning difficulties, this can be extremely difficult. Yet no two children or families are the same and many of the difficulties can indeed be strengths too.

Many children on the autistic spectrum have great attention to detail and become fixed on how to solve a problem, which can be channelled extremely effectively. Greta Thunberg herself attributes her success to her Asperger's.

Keep looking for swaps and ways around problems. My son loves drinking with a straw, so we changed to bamboo ones. Other children will need pull-ups or bedwetting mats for years; try out washable ones, but equally it is important to cut yourself some slack and decide which areas to focus on.

Medication comes with a constant supply of plastic; again, look for ways to recycle or reuse. My son generates additional waste – he cannot always understand that only one print-out is sufficient and meltdowns ensue when demands are not met. Clothes sometimes have to be a specific colour or make.

Remember that every child and family is different. For those with intellectual or physical disabilities, for example, a different approach is needed.

TIPS FOR GREATER INCLUSIVITY AT CHILDREN'S EVENTS

- Be kind and don't judge; every family has their own story, and comments which come across as judgemental can be hurtful.
- When planning an event, consider access and inclusion. Is there scope for wheelchair users to access the beach for a litter pick? Can there be a 'relaxed' version of an event for children and young people with sensory needs? If there is a charge, can recipients of Disabled Living Allowance be given free tickets?
- Find ways into topics which will engage children with learning disabilities. Ocean pollution? Get the *Octonauts* involved! Make it bright and snappy with music and dancing and a catchy song. Find books which appeal to different ages and abilities.

Good books to read with toddlers and pre-schoolers

- **WILD TRIBE HEROES (WWW.WILDTRIBEHEROES.COM)**
A series of books for kids written by Ellie Jackson about plastic pollution and deforestation that are the number one children's book series around these issues. These books are great at connecting the facts with the feelings and tapping into our natural concern for the wildlife and animals impacted by our wasteful ways.
Ages 3+

- *DEAR GREENPEACE*; SIMON JAMES, WALKER BOOKS, 2016
Emily finds a whale living in her pond and writes to Greenpeace for advice. She is undeterred by their advice that a whale can't live in a pond and continues to find out ways to look after her new friend, eventually setting him free.
Ages 3+

- *LIFT-THE-FLAP QUESTIONS AND ANSWERS ABOUT PLASTIC*; KATIE DAYNES AND MARIE-EVE TREMBLAY, USBORNE, 2020
Over 60 interactive flaps to lift to find out about plastic, recycling and how plastic gets into the environment.
Ages 3+

- *10 THINGS I CAN DO TO HELP MY WORLD*; MELANIE WALSH, WALKER BOOKS, 2009
Ten tips for very young children with nice clear simple explanations.
Ages 2+

- *THE BOOK OF BRILLIANT BUGS*; JESS FRENCH AND CLAIRE MCELFATRICK, DK, 2020
This book takes children on a fascinating journey into the world of bugs and creepy crawlies, showing what they do for our planet and how we can help them.
Ages 3+

(Although to be fair, there is very little that is 'quick' with toddlers and pre-schoolers…)

1 Get outside as much as you can This will help your sanity, fill in a bit of time on a looooong day, and will help to develop their love of nature and the outdoors. As frustrating as it is to stop every three seconds to look at specks of dirt on the ground, maybe try to think of it as a mindfulness session…

2 Introduce one new vegetable or fruit a week Just offer it on the side, no pressure. If you're all eating together and they see you tucking in, they might be tempted to try it.

3 Flip the conversation on food waste When they leave something, say something like 'we'll save that for later'. Or, 'we can use that to make some yummy muffins this afternoon' so that they start to see food waste not as waste (if that makes sense).

4 Do a litter pick whenever you go to the park Follow @2minutebeachclean on Instagram for all kinds of 'rubbish inspiration'. The idea is that whenever you go to the beach you spend just two minutes picking up any litter you see. But it doesn't have to just apply to the beach – do it when you go to your local park, or out for a walk.

5 Replace one shop-bought plastic-wrapped snack with a homemade version This doesn't have to involve hours of baking – just chuck some fingers of jam sandwich in a beeswax wrap/bit of foil/Tupperware pot, and give it a go!

Over to you

What will you try? Remember that with kids, it's always going to be trial and error, but have a go. Get curious, see what works and what doesn't. Brainstorm three to four things you could try out and list them below:

Action	Timeframe
1.	
2.	
3.	
4.	

Resources

- **WHIRLI (WWW.WHIRLI.COM)**
  Toy subscription site that means you can keep your kids entertained with 'new' toys, for less cost and less clutter.

- **THE LITTLE LOOP (WWW.THELITTLELOOP.COM)**
  Clothes rental service for bigger kids. At the time of writing, they provide bundles of ethically sourced clothes for ages 2–5 years, and are hoping to expand this to cover from 18 months up to 10 years of age.

- **ECO-CRAFT (WWW.ECO-CRAFT.CO.UK)**
  Great website for recycled card blanks, envelopes, paper sticky tape and lots more.

- **PARTY KIT NETWORK (WWW.PARTYKITNETWORK.UK)**
  Find your nearest party kit to hire (or even start one yourself!).

- **RED TED ART (WWW.REDTEDART.COM)**
  Brilliant website for crafting ideas to do with kids of all ages.

- **SCRAPSTORES**

  Find your nearest one at www.reusefuluk.org

- **LITTLE VEGGIE EATS (@LITTLEVEGGIEEATS)**

  Great book and Instagram feed with easy veggie meals the whole family can eat.

- **LOVE FOOD HATE WASTE (WWW.LOVEFOODHATEWASTE.COM)**

  Website with all kinds of tips, ideas and recipes to help reduce food waste.

- **SEEK APP FROM WWF**

  Download is free onto android or iOS and allows you to identify the wildlife that you spot around you.

- **WILDLIFE WATCH (WWW.WILDLIFEWATCH.ORG.UK)**

  The junior branch of the Wildlife Trusts – some groups have local meet-ups for children, and their website is packed with information and inspiration.

Primary school age kids

Unless you home-school (and if you do, hats off to you – my attempts at home-schooling during the coronavirus crisis in 2020 confirmed my suspicions that it's not for us), that first day at school is a real milestone in our parenting lives, and one that we look back on with a mixture of apprehension, pride and maybe even a tinge of sadness at just how quickly our little ones are growing up. And it brings with it a whole new host of eco-dilemmas…

From the mouths of ~~babes~~ kids...

I don't know about you, but I find it somehow even more heartbreaking to hear directly from kids their worries about the planet. Try asking your kids the three simple questions below and use them as a springboard to help them share any concerns, and any actions you can take together.

Q What do you love about the planet?
A

* 'Animals – they're amazing.' (Earl, age 6)
* 'I love all the wildlife on the planet.' (Lily, age 7)
* 'The variety of nature.' (Freddie, age 10)

Q Is there anything that worries you about the planet and its wildlife?

A

- 'Plastic pollution.' (Sam, age 9)
- 'Because of global warming the Arctic will melt and the planet will become a world of water with no people and no animals.' (Thomas, age 10)
- 'Plastic worries me – there is too much.' (Alina, age 6)

Q Are there any changes you've made to help the planet or wildlife?

A

- 'Go to eco club at school, made a poster for the environment all about how bad plastic straws were – only use metal or paper straws; helped to make an eco brick, WWF – adopted a snow leopard.' (Hannah, age 7)
- 'I go litter picking, put food out for the birds and have a hedgehog house.' (Alina, age 6)
- 'Litter picking.' (Earl, age 6)

School uniform

For children just embarking on their school 'careers', the first trying on of uniform can feel like a momentous (and leaky-eye inducing) moment. Our eldest started school at the very end of our year buying nothing new (it ran from 1st September to 31st August). I ignored the uniform issue for as long as I could, but as September drew closer I had resigned myself to the fact that I would be panic buying the new uniform on the 1st September, the day before school began. But I must have posted something about it on my Facebook page, and arrived back home from an outing somewhere in late August to find a carrier bag of school uniform deposited by our back door. The kindness of that act still makes me feel a little weepy. I had no idea that such things as secondhand uniform services existed up until that point, and certainly no idea that our school had one. But luckily for me, the lady that ran it at the time was a Facebook friend and had seen my plight.

What's so wrong with new school uniforms?

Let me start this with the preface that the most important thing here is that you and your child are happy with their school uniform. If you have no option to choose secondhand, or can't find other eco-friendly possibilities, then please don't feel guilty. Especially when your little one is just starting out at school. It might be that as you find your feet at the school you might feel comfortable suggesting some alternatives to the wider school community, or even getting the PTA on board with a secondhand uniform service. But when you're just starting at a new school it can all feel very daunting (for parents and children alike), and the very last thing I want is to cause you any more anxiety than you already might be feeling as your small person embarks on a big change in all of your lives.

I know some people dislike the concept of school uniforms. Personally I have no issue with it, and like the fact that the only argument we have in the morning over getting dressed for school is quite how long it takes, and that there is no added conflict over what they're going to wear. What I do have issue with is that school uniforms can be the very fastest of fast fashion. Every summer holidays the supermarkets seem to embark on a race to the bottom, of who can provide the cheapest school uniform in the 'back to school' deals. Now I know that school uniform can be expensive, especially if you've got multiple children to buy for, and especially when you factor in shoes, plimsolls, trainers and the pair of wellies they 'must have' to keep in school. And this is where secondhand comes into its own, especially for the (often) non-branded stuff like shorts, pinafores and polo shirts.

Maybe in some cases, school uniforms are a 'loss leader' for some of the supermarkets and they're making very little money on it in order to pass on the savings to customers. Which is great. But it's still bloody cheap. And for clothes to be that cheap, corners need to be cut.

The quality of the materials used will be lower, meaning that they simply won't last to be passed on to younger children, or even see the school year out in some cases.

Cheaper materials will be used, meaning synthetic fabric (made from oil) and cheap cotton, which has a huge water and pesticide footprint. Seam allowances will be next to nothing, meaning that if you're so inclined to try and let down hems to get a little more wear out of them, you're going to be out of luck.

'Stain-resistant' or 'no-iron' clothes are usually coated with plastic (Teflon) to achieve that stain or crease resistance. This plastic coating comes off in tiny particles of microplastics when washed, contributing to the issues of microplastic pollution in the same way that glitter does (see page 109). And it's probably not a great chemical to be wearing next to your skin.

When it comes to labour, corners will also be cut. Sadly, most large clothing retailers just can't be sure who made their clothes, as there is so much sub-contracting of orders along the supply chain. The fast fashion industry is notorious for poor and unsafe working conditions for the women (80 per cent of garment workers are women) who have to work in the industry to provide food for their families. They work long hours in appalling conditions to make our clothes. And sometimes, it might actually be someone else's child making the school uniform for our own. A child who has to sit hunched over a sewing machine, hour after hour, instead of going to school, learning and playing with their friends.

I don't know about you, but that really doesn't sit right with me.

SUSTAINABLE(ISH) OPTIONS FOR TRACKING DOWN SCHOOL UNIFORM

Think secondhand first

Ask to see if your school has a secondhand uniform service. More and more of them do and it's a brilliant way of getting what you need without the financial or eco-burden of new. Our school has one – outgrown uniform is donated, and then sold on for £1 an item. I have managed to kit both of my children out almost entirely using this service, and consequently have probably spent less than £20 on their school uniforms in the last seven years (excluding shoes).

If your school doesn't have this service, don't despair. Ask friends with older kids at the same school, or if you have a class/school Facebook or WhatsApp group, ask in there. Branded stuff is especially hard for people to get rid of when it's outgrown as some charity shops won't take it, so they will probably be delighted to be able to pass it on! For unbranded stuff, do have a look in your local charity shops or on eBay. You should be able to find school trousers and shorts, skirts and pinafores etc. pretty easily.

Another option to have a look at is this website: www.oldschooluniform.co.uk. The idea is that you can buy and sell old school uniform on there, either as an individual, or by getting your school to sign up. It's a great idea in principle, but clearly needs lots of people knowing about it and using it to make it work. So I'm telling you all about it!

Buy ethical

Shopping second-hand for school uniform might not be possible for many reasons. I totally get that when you're busy and your to-do list is threatening to overwhelm you, there are times when you just need to know that you can find the right size/colour/item without having to trawl the charity shops or getting sucked into the politics of the school parents' WhatsApp groups. Fortunately there are a few options that mean you can find ethically produced versions of some of the back to school basics.

Here are some options:

- EcoOutfitters (www.ecooutfitters.co.uk) supply a range of all the school uniform basics made from certified organic cotton and the whole supply chain meets rigorous ethical standards. They are also made to last so with a bit of judicious hemming you might get a good couple of years of wear out of some items, and they'll still be good enough to pass on to siblings and friends.
- KoolSkools (www.koolskools.co.uk) have a range of organic cotton and recycled polyester (made from plastic bottles) uniform, and can provide logo embroidery for schools to register. They also do

Fairtrade 'leavers hoodies' for the obligatory class hoodie as Year 6s move on to secondary school.

- The School Uniform Shop (www.schooluniformshop.co.uk) has been awarded ethical accreditation from The Ethical Company Organisation. They stock a range of brands which all adhere to the company's ethical sourcing policies.

Buy less!

If you ask your parents or grandparents about school uniform, depending on their age you'll probably be regaled with tales of having just one set of school uniform items that had to last them the year. Whether it's because school uniform can now be bought so cheaply, or maybe we wash more (as soon as things are even a teeny bit dirty), or even have less time for washing (so all the kit gets saved up and washed at the weekend), it's not unusual to have a drawer bulging with school uniform.

But in reality, how many of those items are being worn regularly? If my kids are anything to go by, school uniform gets taken off, left on the floor and put back on again the next morning. At which point I will intervene if the jumper is covered in toothpaste (I may start insisting they clean their teeth before they put their uniform on. Always the toothpaste…) or last night's tea (because I can't face the argument that will ensue if I attempt to get them to change out of it after school).

I reckon at a push we could make do with two jumpers, two t-shirts, and one pair of trousers/shorts. But we have way more than that for some reason.

Have a think about your school/working week – how much time you have for sticking on washing, whether it will dry in time etc., and then base your uniform requirements around that.

Also remember to get your kids to try their uniforms on before rushing out and buying new each autumn as a new school year starts. Chances are, a lot of it will still fit, saving you some money, and the planet some precious resources.

Keeping it clean…

Remember that school uniform doesn't have to be pristine, especially at primary school. It's going to be trashed with bits of lunch, paint, and marker pens (*see* opposite), and I honestly don't think teachers really care if jumpers are a bit grubby, or white shirts are a little bit grey. What I'm saying is 'lower your standards'…!

If my kids have got the odd bit of mud or some other stain on their trousers, if I'm organised enough I'll attack it with a damp cloth and sponge it off before leaving it to dry overnight. If I don't see it until we're about to leave the house in the morning, I'll do the same and blast it with the hairdryer to dry it, whilst screeching at the kids to clean their teeth and put their shoes on. #multitasking.

Whenever you can, hang white shirts outside to dry. The sun acts as a natural stain remover and will get out lots of stains that you'd assumed were there to stay.

A squeeze of lemon juice rubbed onto grubby collars before washing can also work wonders.

Ecover do an 'eco-friendly' stain remover which we use and seems to work well on food-based stains, and they also do an eco-friendly laundry bleach for white shirts.

The one thing I haven't found any solution to is the whiteboard marker stains that magic their way onto jumpers and t-shirts. I honestly think that the kids must sometimes sit there drawing on themselves or on each other. And once it's on there, it's on for good. I've given up caring now and send them in wearing their 'personalised' uniform.

SCHOOL SHOES

This is something I've really struggled with and have to confess that we haven't really made any progress. So the eye-wateringly expensive annual (if the foot growing gods choose to shine on you) August trip to the shoe shop still comes with a hefty dose of eco-guilt.

However, I was pleasantly surprised to discover when researching *The Sustainable(ish) Living Guide* that there are indeed some ethical options. However, if you want your kids' feet measured, and the reassurance of a fitting, your options are limited.

Vivobarefoot (www.vivobarefoot.com)

Vivobarefoot make 'barefoot shoes' that are designed to mimic barefoot walking as much as possible and to provide good foot health. They make a range of shoes, including school shoes, and made a commitment that by 2020 they want to be using 90 per cent sustainable materials across their entire product range. They are also aiming to introduce a repair service for all of their shoes, meaning that they will last and last (until they're grown out of!). Sadly, there are only two stores in the UK (London and Edinburgh) so it would be a case of ordering online and making an assessment for fit yourself.

Dr Martens (www.drmartens.com)

Well known for making robust boots and shoes that last the distance, Dr Martens do a range of school shoes for girls and boys, and have a fairly robust set of sustainability policies on their website. It's worth noting that they are a bit more expensive than Clarks, and better for older children who can do laces!

Clarks (www.clarks.co.uk)

It turns out that I can dial my eco-guilt from our annual trip to the Clarks outlet village down a notch or two, as it looks like Clarks are one of the businesses that is starting to take sustainability seriously. From using responsibly sourced leather, through to incorporating an increasing amount of recycled components into their shoes. They have also teamed up with UNICEF to support the education of vulnerable children through a shoe donation scheme.

TREADS (www.treads-shoes.com)

Although I couldn't find any sustainability policies on their website, these shoes are made to last and come with a '12 month indestructible guarantee', so they should see the school year out for even the most energetic of kids. Again, they're only available online, but they have a printable paper measuring gauge and an online size calculator to help, as well as a free returns service.

SCHOOL BAGS

It might be that your school requires at least the younger children to have a branded book bag, and if that's the case your hands are pretty tied unless you can find one secondhand (although both of ours trashed theirs). If however they're free to pick their own, see if you can point them to one of these more ethical options:

- **FRUGI (WWW.WELOVEFRUGI.COM)**

  Perfect for younger children, these bright and colourful backpacks are made from recycled water bottles – it takes seven bottles to make one backpack!

- **PATAGONIA (WWW.EU.PATAGONIA.COM)**

  Patagonia are one of the good guys, and are one of the brands leading the way in sustainability. All of their kit is made to last, and they offer a repair service too. Both of our kids have Patagonia backpacks for school and they're still going strong after several years' use.

- **FJALLRAVEN (WWW.FJALLRAVEN.COM)**

  As well as their popular Kanken backpacks, which are made from recycled bottles, the whole company has robust sustainability policies on their website, along with a whole section on how to care for your bag so it lasts.

Pencil cases and stationery

Who doesn't remember the thrill of the 'back to school' trip to WHSmith to pick out a shiny new pencil case, pencils that didn't have broken leads inside, and that all important unsullied eraser? To be honest though, most kids in primary school don't really need their own pencil case rammed full of their favourite pens and pencils, as everything they need is usually provided for them. If you can't dissuade them, or if your school insists, then look out for pencil cases made from recycled materials (Frugi do ones made from recycled bottles that match their backpacks – *see* above, and there are several available made from recycled tyres).

See page 108 for ideas for more eco-friendly pens and pencils, and remember that they don't need brand new ones every year (no matter how fondly you remember your new pencil cases).

Confession: I still feel the lure of shiny new stationery and have to work hard to resist the appeal of a pretty, pristine notebook and a 'special pen' for every new project.

Plastic-free(ish) packed lunches

School children in the first three years of school in the UK get free hot lunches, which nicely puts off the time until you become a slave to the school lunch box. I have no idea why, but for some reason I find making packed lunches the most soul-destroying activity, and have delegated the task to my husband as he has to make his own lunch to take into work.

Perhaps because I'm not alone in finding it irritatingly time-consuming, there are now a huge number of pre-wrapped things you can find to throw into lunch boxes to make it a whole lot more convenient and less painful. However, these things do come at a cost, to both the pocket and the planet (single-use portions wrapped in largely unrecyclable plastic).

The bad news here is that unless you can delegate the task to your partner, I can't make packed lunches any less soul-destroying, but I can help you to make them a teeny bit less planet-destroying.

LUNCH BOXES

Buy to last would be my advice (again!) here. We've been through a fair number of plastic lunch boxes that seem to break or split.

- Huski (www.huskihome.com) do a lunch box made from recycled rice husks that has two compartments and holds hot or cold food.
- Elephant Box (www.elephantbox.co.uk) produce a range of stainless steel lunch boxes and snack pots that are designed to be robust and to last.
- Frugi (www.welovefrugi.com) do a lunch bag to complement their backpacks (*see* page 137) that's also made from recycled bottles, has two zipped compartments, and even a cloud nametag.

ALTERNATIVES TO CLINGFILM

Clingfilm is so easy and so versatile, isn't it? But it's a single-use plastic and because it's often contaminated with the food that was wrapped in it, it's really hard to recycle. Fortunately there are lots of easy to use alternatives:

Beeswax wraps

The internet LOVES beeswax wraps and they are on every zero-waste bloggers list of essential swaps. They are essentially pieces of fabric that have been coated with beeswax (or soy wax for vegans) that then become pliable and stick together, so can be used in a similar way to clingfilm. You can use them to wrap your sandwiches, piece of cake, or to fold up and create little snack pouches for things like crisps or chopped fruit. They are widely available online, and they're also stocked in places like Waitrose and Lakeland. Alternatively, if you want to save some money and are feeling crafty, you can buy 'make your own kits', or simply source some beeswax and have a go yourself.

TOP TIPS FOR BEESWAX WRAPS

- Don't wash in hot water – the beeswax melts and disappears! Simply wipe with a damp cloth and leave to dry.
- If they start to lose their stick, they can be rejuvenated by sprinkling with beeswax pellets and ironing (have a look online for instructions).
- Remind your kids to save them and bring them home again (ours have managed this so far!).

Foil

Train your kids not to scrunch up the foil, and then you can give it a wipe down and reuse it until it starts to disintegrate. At which point it can be recycled.

Top tip – foil needs to be scrunched together with other foil until it's the size of a tennis ball before it goes in your recycling bin/box, otherwise it can be too small for the recycling grabber things (technical term) to detect it.

Tupperware

We LOVE Tupperware in our house. Yes it's plastic, but it's not single use. You don't need to go splashing out on expensive new stuff – old margarine or ice-cream tubs, and takeaway containers will work just as well.

Top tip – if you can devise a system that keeps the appropriate lid with the correct bottom, you should market it and make your fortune. Only after you've shared your secret with me…

YOGHURTS

If your kids like taking a yoghurt or a yoghurt tube to school, then you can still do this with less plastic. For a long time we used to decant yoghurt from a 500ml pot into a mini Tupperware pot and pack this into the kids lunch boxes with a spoon, and this worked really well. For no apparent reason that I can remember (other than feeling vaguely guilty when my kids would come home excitedly telling of the kids who had Frubes and could just suck their yoghurt straight out of the pack…) I ordered some Doddlebags (*see* page 85) and we now portion out yoghurt from large pots into these bags.

SNACKS

If it was down to me, I would quite happily sacrifice crisps to reduce a little bit of our plastic footprint. Sadly however, the family have rejected my calls for a benign dictatorship where I get to make all the decisions, and are not at all on board with being a crisp-free house. Our compromise therefore is to buy the big share bags, and to dole out a handful into their lunch boxes. These either go in a sandwich bag that gets reused, or in a separate compartment in their lunch boxes.

The temptation with snacks can be to buy all the single-wrapped packs of biscuits, cakes, malt loaf slices etc., but this can add up to a LOT of plastic. There are some ideas for easy plastic-free homemade snacks on page 118 that can be made in batches and stashed in the freezer. But if you really can't face it/don't have the time or energy, then buy the biggest sizes you can find, or cut into child-sized portions which are then either wrapped in a beeswax wrap, or popped into some Tupperware.

WATER BOTTLES

Across the world, a million plastic bottles are produced every single minute, and 7 billion are used each year in the UK. A reusable water bottle is a super easy swap, and not just for school. Here are three of the best:

1 **Chilly's Bottles (www.chillysbottles.com)**
We've got one of these each, and we all love them. They keep cold drinks really nice and cold all day long in the summer, and have survived being dropped and bashed around in school bags.

2 **Klean Kanteen (www.kleankanteen.co.uk)**
Klean Kanteen have a 'Kid Kanteen' range alongside their regular bottles, which are smaller and come with either a sports cap, a sippy cap, or a regular cap.

3 **Pura Bottles (www.purastainless.co.uk)**
These are the bottles mentioned in the baby feeding section on page 77 that are stainless steel and have interchangeable lids that grow with your kids. They come with the option of an insulated sleeve and a choice of bottle lids.

> **DID YOU KNOW?**
> If water bottles start to smell a bit fusty, or acquire a 'taint' from flavoured drinks, fill with water, add a teaspoon of bicarbonate of soda and leave to stand overnight.

JUICE AND SMOOTHIES

If your little one is used to having a box of juice in their lunch box, try these reusable 'drink in a box' containers with integral straws (www.ekokids.co.uk/products/drink-in-the-box). Alternatively, the 'squeasy snacker' on page 85 can also be used for drinks and juice. If you really can't give up the cartons, then make sure they bring them home and you recycle them if you can (some councils will take tetrapacks with their kerbside recycling).

Greening your school

School is a place that most of our children spend a lot of time, and it can have a big influence on the way they see the world. With a packed curriculum and continually shifting goal-posts, it can be easy to see how 'eco stuff' might fall down, or even off, the list of priorities. But there's a growing awareness amongst schools both of the changes they can make on site, as well as the crucial role they play in equipping our children with the information, skills and resources they will need as they grow up in a rapidly changing climate.

At the time of writing over 18,500 schools (about 60 per cent of all UK schools) are registered with Eco-Schools England, who have this to say on their website:

'The Eco-Schools programme is an ideal way for schools to embark on a meaningful path towards improving the environment in both the school and the local community while at the same time having a life-long positive impact on the lives of young people and their families.'

Sometimes it just needs one passionate person – whether that's a teacher, governor, teaching assistant, or PTA member – to take it on and make things happen. And that one person could be you!

5 TOP TIPS FOR GETTING YOUR SCHOOL ON BOARD

1 Don't go in with all guns blazing, criticising the school for its lack of eco-initiatives (not that any of you lovely readers would do this I'm sure). Sound out a couple of the teachers first and ask them if anything has been done/trialled before.
2 Check out the Eco-Schools website so that you've got a really clear idea of the resources and support available, and what might be expected of the school, the staff and the pupils.
3 Be prepared for the fact that you might be the one who is asked to lead on any action, or at least to liaise with a designated member of staff. Offer to run an assembly, or an after-school eco club. Remember that you absolutely do NOT need to be an 'expert' or to have all the answers. You just need to be passionate, enthusiastic and open to learning.

4 See if you can get some other parents on board. If you've got a class Facebook or WhatsApp group, ask in there if anyone else is interested. Or if they think their kids would be up for an eco-club or similar.
5 Focus on the other benefits that being more eco-friendly brings to the school: cost savings on energy, resources and waste; increased links with the community; pupil power and citizenship. Ofsted are also fans.

10 EASY WAYS TO GREEN UP YOUR SCHOOL

1 Water fountains – ensure that all the children and staff are encouraged to have their own refillable water bottles and know where they can re-fill them from in school.
2 Double check what can be recycled with either the local authority or whoever has the recycling contract for the school – make sure that all the recycling bins are clearly labelled, and that they are easy to access. Sometimes putting a box for paper recycling in each classroom can really help to stop it going into the bin.
3 Do weekly litter picks – this can easily be turned into a maths lesson looking at how many items are collected, what types of rubbish are collected, and comparing week on week figures. There's also a great geography lesson to be had on how plastic ends up in the rivers and oceans and the damage it does, as well as a spot of citizenship/activism writing to the brands to ask them what they are doing to help prevent plastic pollution.
4 Energy saving – some schools have pupil eco-monitors whose 'job' it is to go round the classrooms making sure all the lights and electrical equipment is switched off. This might not sound like it will make a massive difference, but when you learn that leaving one computer on overnight for a year generates enough CO_2 to fill a double-decker bus, you realise it actually does!
5 Idling cars at school drop-off and pick-up – this drives me mad, but I am still never quite brave enough to march up to the window and ask people to turn their engines off. I serve up my very best

'Paddington stare' instead, and tut loudly, but I'm not sure how useful that is. One minute of idling produces 150 balloons of harmful pollutants. Right into the very air that our children are walking past, or outside their playground.

Our school got the kids to design posters and then tied them to the playground fence, which I thought was really clever and hopefully much more powerful and motivating than simple finger wagging from the school. If all else fails, you might be able to enlist the help of the local Police Community Support Officers to do a bit of patrolling.

6 Swap school milk in plastic bottles or tetrapacks for glass bottles. If your school uses Cool Milk for their free milk for under fives, then I'm told that it's really quite simple to contact them and ask for the milk to be provided in glass bottles instead. They will even supply washable cups, and take the empty glass bottles back to reuse.

7 Outdoor space. How can the outdoor space be utilised to create more biodiversity? This can be as simple as getting the kids involved in creating bug hotels (*see* page 122) or leaving some areas of the school field unmown to create wildlife spaces.

8 Food waste. Collecting all of the food waste from a week's (or even a day's) school dinners is a great way to start a conversation with the children about food waste, where it goes, and the impact it has on the planet. Some schools have their own wormeries, or even their own mini bio-digesters to deal with their food waste.

9 Plastic-free packed lunches – aim to have a day a week, or a focus week, where the parents and children are encouraged to either attempt a plastic-free lunch box, or to swap one single-use plastic item for a reusable one. Parents need to be given plenty of notice on this one, as well as signposted to easy and affordable alternatives – can you imagine anything worse than being told by your child at 8am that morning that their lunch box needs to be plastic-free that day?!

10 Reduce/eliminate single-use plastic within the school. Do the children really need glitter when they're crafting? Can paper tape be swapped in for Sellotape? Can you get refillable glue sticks?

IDEAS FOR A 'ZERO WASTE(ISH) PTA'

If you're on the PTA (or even if you're not) you might be dismayed at the amount of plastic tat that seems to abound at events. From endless mini packets of Haribo to glow sticks for the school disco, it's everywhere. And sometimes it can feel like selling plastic tat, or plastic-encrusted crafts made by the kids, is the easiest way to raise funds. But fear not, there are lots of easy tweaks that can be made, and lots of effective fundraisers that don't involve exploiting the planet to raise funds for our school.

Secondhand uniform service.

I've extolled the virtues of this already (*see* page 132) as a more planet-friendly way to kit our kids out for school, but it can also be quite a good fundraiser.

Cake sales

We have one of these every half-term at school, with each year group taking it in turn to bake and man the stall. It's always hugely popular and raises around £150 each time, so nearly £1000 per year! Ask parents to bring in Tupperware to take their cake slices home in, and have a stash of paper bags ready for those who forget.

Secondhand book sale

Ask families to have a clear-out of books that are no longer read and sell them one afternoon in the playground after school.

Toy/game swap

Again, ask families to have a clear-out and then lay everything out in the school hall. The children pay a small entry fee to come in, browse the toys and then take away x number of items each.

Jam jar tombola

Ask families to bring in an empty jam jar filled with something nice for a kids tombola. You can stipulate that it has to be plastic-free, and give suggestions such as hair clips, pick 'n' mix style sweets, crayons etc.

Some easy changes our PTA has made

I raised my concerns with our school PTA (I may have been chair of it at the time!) about the glow sticks (single use and full of chemicals and packaged in yet more plastic) that we were selling at the school disco. The kids loved them, and they were quite a good money spinner, but I was pleasantly surprised to find that other people shared my concerns. We simply decided not to do them – we didn't replace them with anything else, we just didn't sell them. And I didn't hear one complaint from the kids. Also, instead of selling individual packs of Haribo and chocolate bars at school events, we buy the giant jars of pick 'n' mix sweets and bag them up into paper bags, and when we do film nights we buy giant sacks of popcorn from our local cinema and dispense it in bowls.

DRESS-UP DAYS

God I feel like such an old curmudgeon, but I really hate dress-up days. The pressure to conjure up an outfit, usually at pretty short notice, that your child will actually wear is immense. And it's easy to see why many of us turn to Amazon or the local supermarket to help bail us out.

But 'World Book Day' costumes, or nativity outfits, along with Halloween costumes and Christmas jumpers can be the very fastest of fast fashion. They are usually literally made to be worn only once or twice, are entirely synthetic (made from plastic), and often coated in chemicals to make them flame retardant.

If I had to single one out as the one that irritates me the most, it's World Book Day. Don't get me wrong – I love the *idea* of World Book Day, and anything that gets kids excited about books and reading is a Good Thing. I just hate the need to dress up for it. Or more specifically the fact that time-poor parents faced with yet another thing to cram into their lives will probably just hit Amazon or the supermarket for a mass-produced plastic monstrosity that will be worn once and then condemned to landfill to sit for centuries to come. When you can pick up a costume that looks about a gazillion times better than anything you could cobble together yourself at home, for less than a tenner, why would you go to the hassle of trying to make a papier mâché spaceman's helmet, or forage the woods for sticks to make a bonafide witch's broomstick?

But all of these super cheap, and super convenient costumes, are like all of our clothes – the raw materials had to come from somewhere (usually oil as most of these are synthetic fabrics) and have to be made by someone. They aren't magicked out of thin air by machines. Real people will have sewn every seam. Soooo ... how can we send your little darlings to school in costumes that haven't cost the earth?

Reuse

If you've already got a costume from previous parties, nativity plays, World Book Days, or Halloween, drag it out and use it again. Chances are your kids can't even remember what they went as last time, let alone any of their friends.

Borrow

Ask around friends and family if they have a costume you can borrow. We have a class Facebook group, and everyone shared in there what outfits they had, or what they were looking for. There's no need to go and buy an Alice in Wonderland or a shepherd's outfit – chances are someone you know already has one. I saw a post on Facebook where someone said their school was having a 'costume swap shop' in the run-up to World Book Day, and again for nativity – this is GENIUS!

Recycle/upcycle

Have a quick scout around the charity shops and see what you can find. I once found a fake fur gilet thing that has been an Asterix outfit, and this year is going to be re-utilised for our youngest to be 'Hiccup the Horrendous Haddock III' from *How to Train your Dragon*. You honestly don't need to be an expert at sewing either – very basic hand sewing is all that's required, or failing that getting happy with a glue gun...

Go easy

My strategy for World Book Day tends to be to think of a character from a book that we've read recently that requires minimal dressing up or a costume we already have, and then to suggest heavily that this is who they might like to go as. It usually works and I sit there feeling smug until about 8pm the night before when they change their minds…

Sports equipment/outdoor gear/ bikes etc.

These days, once kids start primary school it feels like the race is on to enrich their education and get them signed up to as many after-school clubs as possible. And not only do they take up a huge amount of time and energy, they usually need a shed load (quite literally if that's where you end up storing it all!) of stuff. Whether it's Cubs and Brownies, swimming lessons, football, ballet, or even a family bike ride, it all seems to need an entirely different set of clothes at the very least.

BORROW DON'T BUY

At least to start with. If your kids are desperate to start a new club or sport, see if you can borrow what you need until you know that they're going to stick with it. Many clubs will have a stash of football boots, or hockey sticks, or whatever it is you need to borrow for the first few tries. Or ask friends if they have any kit you can use for a short period of time.

Think secondhand first

With kids growing as quickly as they do, kit often gets outgrown before it's really been used very much – especially if it's only a weekly club. We've picked up astro boots for hockey in pretty much new condition from eBay, and I reckon if we'd looked harder we would have been able to find Cubs t-shirts secondhand quite easily.

BIKES

Ah, nothing quite beats a family bike ride. As long as it's less than 2 miles, you have drinks for everyone, snacks for bribing them to carry on, have stopped every 35 seconds to take off jumpers, put on jumpers, check saddle heights, and have double panniers on each adult's bike to carry all the required snacks and discarded jumpers. It's a such a joy…

I jest. Kind of. We actually do really enjoy a bike ride, and if the stars align we can on occasion make it a reasonable distance with minimal whinging #parentinggoals.

Being able to ride a bike is one of those things that feels like a life skill our kids should all have. And hopefully if policy changes are bought in that limit cars in city centres, cycling will become a more and more popular way to travel and commute.

The usual advice to borrow or to look secondhand applies here – especially for things like bike seats and trailers that will only be used for relatively short periods of time.

Tag-a-longs

We found a tag-a-long called a 'Trailgator' (www.trail-gator.com) that could be used with the kids normal bikes. They could be hooked up for busier roads and hills, and then 'let loose' on quiet flat roads to practise their cycling. It meant we didn't have to buy a special tag-a-long bike that was only used for a short period of time and the kids really liked the chance of having a bit of freedom and independence when we were off-road.

Balance bikes

Both of ours started off their cycling journeys on balance bikes, and I absolutely love them. We were gifted a Wishbone bike (www.uk.wishbonedesign.com) by my parents, which has taught both our kids the balance needed to quickly (within hours/days) get the hang of a 'proper bike' when the time came to make the transition. It's now been passed on to their younger cousins and is doing sterling service for them.

As always, see if you can borrow one from a friend, or look for one secondhand. The toy subscription service Whirli (www.whirli.com – *see* page 97) have balance bikes available, which might be a good way to see if your child is keen to use one before investing.

Kids' bikes

We've managed to find all of the kids' bikes so far secondhand. After a spot of research, hubby set his heart on getting them Isla bikes (www.islabikes.co.uk), which are lightweight and specifically designed for the different needs of children at different growth stages. They make their bikes to last, and are also working on the 'Imagine Project' where bikes will be rented, not owned, and they have a closed loop system, where none of the resources or materials are wasted and are all reused at the end of a bike's life. Because they're such good quality, it's both easy to find them secondhand and then sell them on again once they're outgrown.

> ### DID YOU KNOW?
> The Bike Club (www.thebikeclub.co.uk) is a monthly subscription service for kids bikes, starting from balance bikes and going up to mountain and road bikes for older children. You pay a monthly subscription depending on the size and make of the bike, and once the bike is outgrown you simply exchange it for the next size up!

The school run

Unless you home-school your kids, there is no getting away from the school run, and around 46 per cent of primary school pupils are driven to school.

In an experiment performed by the BBC in 2019, they compared the pollution levels experienced by families on the same school run, using three different modes of transport: on foot, on bike and in the car. The results showed that those in the car were exposed to the highest levels of pollution (44 per cent over the WHO recommended limit), compared to 40.1 per cent for those walking and 28.1 per cent for the family who cycled. This happens because the air from outside (containing all the fumes from the cars in front) comes into the car and is trapped inside. So our perception that the car is the safest place to be, might not be the case, especially when it comes to levels of air pollution.

> Confession: We drive to school every day, and I feel really crappy about it. In my defence we do have an electric car, but as I've tried explaining to the kids, that doesn't make it a guilt-free option – it still adds to the traffic clogging up the road outside school, causing more idling cars to spew out more fumes.
>
> I would love to cycle, but my kids it appears, would very much not. We tried it once and it ended in tears (the youngest's, and very nearly mine) and we scraped into school with a minute to spare and one very bad-tempered child (the other one wasn't so bothered). I haven't been brave enough to try again.

So what are the sustainable(ish) options?

WALK OR SCOOT

If you're lucky to live close enough, then clearly walking or scooting is the thing to do. If you're worried about traffic, wear high vis jackets, and make sure you always position yourself between the kids and the road.

BIKE

I would LOVE to cycle to school but, as I've said, my kids have other ideas, and to my shame I haven't had the energy (or resilience to tantrums) to push it. However, I do think that if I had known about cargo bikes when they were younger I would have given them some serious consideration. There are all kinds of models available now that allow you to transport the kids either in front of you, or behind, and there's even the option of electric versions so that you don't have to arrive at the school gate red faced and sweating.

When I wrote *The Sustainable(ish) Living Guide* I approached the walking and cycling charity Sustrans to see if they would share some tips for safer cycling with kids, and Chris Bennett, their Head of Behaviour Change, kindly shared some, which I'll summarise here:

- It doesn't have to be all or nothing – swapping just a couple of journeys from car to bike can still make a big difference.
- If your children aren't yet old enough to cycle safely, then look at options like box-style cargo bikes which are ideal for transporting young children around.
- Once your child is confident on their bike, get them used to riding on the roads. For those needing that extra confidence boost, there are courses like Bikeability which teach valuable skills, such as good road positioning, signalling and visibility, and can help parents and children feel at ease on busy streets.
- Ride in a line with the children in the middle for maximum safety, or if there is only one adult, take up a position at the back so that you can clearly see all the children.

BUS

Most schools have a bus service for children to use, that is either available solely for the school children, or that has adult chaperones on board to ensure everyone's safety. Again, it doesn't have to be all or nothing – if you still want that contact at the school gate and in the playground, could your kids get the bus a couple of times a week?

CAR

If you have to drive, consider the following:

- Can you park a little further away and walk the remainder, reducing congestion (and fumes) outside the school gate?
- Don't idle! Turn your engine off when you're waiting outside school.

- Can you lift share with another family who live close to you? Maybe not all the time, but once a week (or more)?
- If you are looking to buy a new car, then do seriously look into electric. The price is coming down all the time, at the same time as the ranges you can drive on a full charge are going up (we can get 280 miles on a charge from our Kia e-Niro).

Holidays

I very clearly remember being told by a friend with older children that going on holiday with young kids was simply 'doing the same shit in a different place' and not quite believing her. Until we went on holiday with our young kids. And then realised that holidays as we knew them were a thing of the past.

Nevertheless, a change can be as good as a rest, as the saying goes, and most of us will endeavour to venture away from home with our kids at least once a year. Flight-free holidays are the way to go if you're looking for low-carbon holiday options, although not always the way to go when looking for guaranteed sunshine. However, flight-free doesn't have to mean you're confined to the British Isles (although there is a strong argument that we have some of the finest history, culture and scenery in the world, so why would you look anywhere else? Except maybe the weather…). I know lots of families who drive down to the south of France each year, or who get the Eurostar to Paris, Brussels and beyond. You can also get the ferry to the Netherlands, and then access their brilliant network of (very flat) cycleways.

Someone without kids told me that the key to flight-free travel was seeing the journey as a part of the holiday and the experience, but as I say, she didn't have kids. And I totally get that for those of us who have, we can feel quite anxious to get the travelling bit over and done with. However, it is more do-able than you might think.

We've driven up to Scotland several times with ours, towing our caravan, and stopped overnight on the way up and on the way back. We managed this largely thanks to Percy Pigs and the entire Harry Potter audiobook collection.

But don't just take my word for it – here's some 'real world' advice from people who've travelled long distances with their kids in tow.

George

We've gone ferry and car to the Netherlands and south of France several times. The ferry part is easy and fun. Netherlands was very quick and no trouble at all – only one loo stop! The journey to the south of France was very long but they have lovely service stops everywhere serving decent food or just coffee, always with playgrounds. We had a bag of toys that were released hourly, lots of movies and car games. Hard but much easier than flying!

Jenny

I interrailed to Italy when the children were in primary school. Overnight train from Paris to Venice was exciting! Main recommendations are to book seats round a table for games and easier eating, make use of left luggage for times between accommodation check-out and train departure, and to alternate 'tourist/monument/church/art' type days with beach/local swimming pool days. I really like train travel for the space it gives you.

Cass

When we lived in the UK we drove to Austria every year with the kids. Took the Chunnel. Plenty of snacks, breaking up the journey as needed and had a 'no tech until after lunch' rule so they did eye-spy and other family games in the morning and then we all got some peace and quiet in the afternoon. Now living in the US, so long car journey/road trips are more normal. Last summer we drove from Boston into Canada and stayed at some amazing national parks.

ON THE BEACH

Visiting the beach is pretty much a 'must do' for the summer holidays for us Brits – whether we're having a staycation or just enjoying a day trip. Regardless of the weather, you will find us there, determinedly enjoying ourselves, wearing varying layers of clothing depending on the temperature.

But sadly, we tend to leave behind 'more than footprints' when we visit the beach. Litter on the beach gets washed in from the sea but also gets left there by daytrippers, and then becomes not only an eyesore but a danger to the wildlife in the area as well. One thing we can all do is to join in with a #2minutebeachclean – a movement started by Martin Dorey, a writer, surfer and anti-plastic campaigner. Simply spend two minutes picking up any litter you see and deposit it in the nearest bin (or take it home with you if there isn't a bin). If you're so inclined you can take a pic of your mini beach clean and its results and share on social media with the #2minutebeachclean hashtag. That hashtag has been shared over 130,000 times on Instagram and there are now dedicated #2minutebeachclean boards at many of the UK's beaches with litter pickers and bags to help you to do your bit.

No trip to the beach would be complete without a bucket and spade, but how many times have you bought a cheap version, only for it to break after just a couple of uses? The old mantra 'buy less, buy better' works very well in this scenario – there are several more robust and eco-friendly versions out there made from plant-based plastics. Yes, they are more expensive (they would make a great gift suggestion though!) but with just a little bit of care they could be the only bucket you need for years to come. Try a 'scrunch bucket' – flexible silicon buckets that save space and won't crack!

Body boards are another big issue for beach waste – River Care, an organisation run by Keep Britain Tidy and Anglian Water, picked up 600 broken and discarded polystyrene body boards from three beaches in the space of just one month. And every year thousands of them are dumped on the beach, often after just one use. According to Surfers Against Sewage, the answer is to either buy a new or secondhand quality board that will last. Or if it's your first time having a go, many surf shops and beach stores now have rental schemes where you can hire a good quality, plastic-free board for the duration of your holiday.

And my favourite 'zero waste' tip for beach trips (and pretty much any trip anywhere if the sun is vaguely shining) is to get your ice-cream in a cone and not a cup, meaning you can scoff ice-cream and polish your eco-halo simultaneously.

Is flying really that bad?

In short, yes. A plane ticket is about the most carbon-intensive thing you can buy as an individual.

- Aviation currently makes up around 2–4 per cent of global greenhouse gas emissions.
- Only around 5 per cent of the world's population actually use aeroplanes.
- The US, China and the EU account for 55 per cent of all aviation-based emissions.
- Brits fly more than any nation – twice as much as Americans.
- On an individual level, there is no other human activity that emits as much carbon over such a short period of time as aviation.

But does that mean that we should never set foot on a plane again, and that I'm expecting you to forgo your hard-earned annual week in the sun? No it doesn't. Because this is sustainable(ish).

However, we do need to reassess our relationship with flying and in the same way as we're trying to consume more thoughtfully, think about how we can fly more thoughtfully instead. So instead of hopping on to a plane for a short business trip, could you Skype or Zoom instead? Instead of jetting off to Prague for a hen/stag-do, could you have just as much pre-wedding fun in Blackpool or Brighton?

The coronavirus pandemic of 2020 showed us just how many business meetings could actually be done easily online, for a fraction of the carbon emissions and time involved in in-person meetings – hopefully something that companies will learn from and continue to embrace moving forwards.

What about carbon off-setting?

Carbon off-setting is a way to compensate for your emissions by paying for an equivalent carbon dioxide saving somewhere else. One concern when using it for flights is that it can feel like a bit of a 'get out of jail free' card and like we can carry on jetting off all over the world with a clear conscience because we're off-setting.

However, if you've thought about other options, and for whatever reason they aren't viable, carbon off-setting your fights is better than not! Make sure you research the scheme thoroughly and look out for 'Gold Standard' schemes. The World Land Trust (www.worldlandtrust.org) is endorsed by David Attenborough and, importantly, works to protect existing carbon sinks and rainforest, rather than simply planting trees.

HOW TO BE A SUSTAINABLE(ISH) TOURIST

However you travel, once you get to your destination, remember all the basic principles around reuse and recycling. Resist the urge to stick to the familiar brands and support local independent shops and cafes whenever you can.

1 Take public transport once at your destination if possible instead of hiring a car.
2 Try to eat local and seasonal produce.
3 Look for 'low carbon' activities to do, e.g. rock climbing over something like jet skiing which uses a lot of fuel over a short period of time.
4 Shop locally – if you're looking for souvenirs to take home, choose independent artisan crafts over novelty t-shirts.
5 Take reusable water bottles wherever you go. If the water isn't safe to drink at your destination (or as you're travelling to get there) you might have to rely on bottled, but have a look at Water-to-Go (www.watertogo.eu), which is a portable water filtration system that 'eliminates over 99.9 per cent of all microbiological contaminants'.

Raising eco-aware kids – part 2

(*See* page 121 for part 1.)

Most primary schools will include at least some teaching around aspects of being 'eco-friendly', whether that's learning about plastics and recycling, or having a 'climate week'. So it's likely that your kids will have some awareness of the issues facing the planet.

Obviously primary school covers a wide range of ages, and within that, levels of understanding about the wider world. With the younger children, very much follow the ideas given for toddler and pre-schoolers on page 121. Keep it local, and encourage a love of nature. As children get older you might find that they start asking questions that you don't really feel equipped to answer, or that indeed you don't have any answers for. We had one teary bedtime with my eldest when he asked why humans were doing what they were doing and causing the ice to melt. I didn't have an answer for him, and I still don't. But I think it's really important that we acknowledge our children's fears and anxieties, even if it taps into our own. Sometimes saying 'I don't know' can be the most honest answer we have. But then point them to the hope. Tell that you don't know, but what you do know is that there are a whole bunch of people, scientists, politicians, campaigners, working really hard and doing everything they can to help protect the planet and its wildlife.

Focus on action. Focus on things that they can do, that you can do as a family. As an adult it's really easy to feel hopeless and disempowered around these issues, so I can only imagine how it must feel as a child. One thing I did with our eldest after a traumatic viewing of one of the episodes of David Attenborough's *One Planet Seven Worlds* series was sit with him and help him to brainstorm ideas of things that he could do to help, as a then 10-year-old. He didn't necessarily go and do all of them, but it helped him to realise that he really could make a difference.

This is what we came up with (obviously adapt this to the age of your child):

1 Draw posters and share them – ask school if he can put one up, and he asked me if I could share it on social media for him.
2 Write to politicians, and send them a copy of his poster.
3 Fundraise for charities like the World Wildlife Fund or the local Wildlife Trust through activities such as a table-top sale, a sponsored walk/bike ride, selling unwanted toys at a car boot/on eBay or a sponsored litter pick.
4 Ask school if they would consider holding an after school 'climate club' one term.
5 Join in with the next student climate strike, and write a letter to his headmistress explaining why he feels it's so important.

6 Speak to school about becoming an Eco-School.

7 Do a litter pick or a #2minutebeachclean.

8 Do our best to remember our reusable plastic items and avoid single-use plastic wherever we can.

9 Read labels and make informed decisions around palm oil – I'm going to introduce him to the Giki app (www.Giki.earth) and let him loose scanning the foodstuffs in our kitchen.

10 Talk to his friends about how he's feeling and some of the easy changes we're making as a family (as adults there's a conversation we need to have with our children around judgement and ensuring they're not 'telling people off' before we encourage them to talk to others though).

Palm oil

Palm oil is used in a huge variety of products from food through to cosmetics. Every hour, 300 football fields of precious remaining forest are being ploughed to the ground across South East Asia to make way for palm oil plantations, meaning that this vital ecosystem is lost forever.

However, it's not a clear-cut situation (when is it ever?) as palm oil is a hugely productive crop – it produces 4–10 times more oil per unit of land than comparable crops like soy or rapeseed. So if we were to simply swap palm oil for another oil, even more land would be needed.

What we need is to ensure that there are robust certifications in place to make sure that palm oil is being produced in a sustainable way that isn't contributing to deforestation. As consumers we can let manufacturers know that we want them to source sustainable palm oil with robust sustainability certifications. And we can consume less – the rise in popularity of palm oil has come about in some part in response to the demand for processed food. Cooking from scratch when you can and reducing consumption of highly processed foods (also good for our health) is a great way to avoid inadvertently consuming palm oil. Remember again that it doesn't have to be all or nothing.

School strikes

It's worth saying that despite the odd tearful conversation and making a poster or two, my kids have remained fairly un-engaged with climate action. I'm not sure whether they just feel like it's 'mum's thing', or maybe they trust that I've got it all in hand... I've asked them several times if they want to go along to one of the local school strikes, but each time they've looked at me like I was slightly mad. And yes, I feel a little bit frustrated and in some ways a bit like I'm failing in my duty to bring up politically engaged and active young people. But then I remind myself that they're only 11 and 9, and quite rightly their attention is more on Lego and Minecraft than it is on the potential end of civilisation as we know it.

If your kids are keen and engaged, then encourage and support them. Take them along to climate strikes if they want to go, help them take the action that they want to. But if they aren't that bothered, don't push it. Yes, they need to know about this stuff, but when the time is right for them. In the same way that all adults aren't engaging around the climate crisis, some kids won't too. And that's OK. All we can do is model some eco-friendly practices, keep lines of communication open, and empower them as much as we can that their actions do make a difference.

(For more on school strikes *see* page 192.)

Books for superhero kids who want to save the planet

- *KIDS FIGHT PLASTIC: HOW TO BE A #2MINUTESUPERHERO;
  MARTIN DOREY, WALKER BOOKS, 2019*
  Written by Martin Dorey, founder of the #2minutebeachclean
  movement, this book gives kids (and their parents!)
  50 'missions' to help reduce plastic in their homes, at school
  and on days out.

- *101 SMALL WAYS TO CHANGE THE WORLD*; AUBRE ANDRUS, LONELY PLANET KIDS, 2018

    This book from Lonely Planet Kids shows that you're never too young to make a big difference, and 'includes random acts of kindness, craft projects, energy-saving ideas and much more.' I haven't got a copy (yet) but it sounds wonderfully action orientated and very practical!

- *PLASTIC SUCKS!*; DOUGIE POYNTER, MACMILLAN CHILDREN'S BOOKS, 2019

    Written by Dougie Poynter of McFly fame, this book is really good fun! I've got a copy and have just started reading it with our nine-year-old and it seems to be holding his attention. It covers some of the history of how we got where we are now, as well as some of the inspiring projects that are happening around the globe, and of course, what we can be doing at home.

- *WHAT A WASTE: RUBBISH, RECYCLING, AND PROTECTING OUR PLANET*; JESS FRENCH, DK CHILDREN, 2019

    Jess French is a vet and presenter of the CBeebies *Minibeast Adventure*. In this book is 'everything you need to know about what we're doing to our environment, good and bad, from pollution and litter to renewable energy and plastic recycling'. As well as explaining how things are going wrong, I love that it also shows what we're doing right, and inspires with some awesome tales of positivity.

- *BE PLASTIC CLEVER*; AMY AND ELLA MEEK, DK, MAY 2020

    Written by teenagers Amy and Ella Meek, this book not only teaches young activists about the dangers of plastic pollution and climate change but also helps them to find their own voice.

5 QUICK WINS WITH PRIMARY SCHOOL KIDS

1 **See how much of their school uniform you can find secondhand** Not only will this help to save the planet, it will potentially save you a stack of cash too.

2 **Swap out one single-use plastic item in lunch boxes** Pick the thing that will be easiest, and ask your kids for suggestions for replacements to try and make sure they're on board and don't mutiny…

3 **Have one car-free school run a week** Whether that's the bus, or cycling, is there a way you can get everyone to school without using the car? Or can you car share with another family?

4 **Make sure everyone has a reusable water bottle** And remembers to take it out with them!

5 **Offer to hold an assembly at your kids' school** Please please please believe me when I said you don't need to be an expert. I did 10 minutes at my kids' school, talking about 'The Big Four' single-use plastics (*see* page 26) and took in some of my reusables to show them. They were so engaged and full of ideas, it was wonderful to see.

Over to you

What will you try? Sit down with the kids and ask them if there's anything they want to try. Brainstorm three to four things you could have a go at as a family and list them below:

Action	Timeframe
1.	
2.	
3.	
4.	

Resources

- **ECO-SCHOOLS (WWW.ECO-SCHOOLS.ORG.UK)**
  Packed with resources, information and support for schools looking to become more planet friendly.

- **SURFERS AGAINST SEWAGE, PLASTIC-FREE SCHOOLS (WWW.SAS. ORG.UK/PLASTIC-FREE-SCHOOLS)**
  A pupil-led education programme from the marine protection charity, designed to equip pupils with tools and challenges that create positive, lasting environmental change.

- **TED ED (WWW.ED.TED.COM)**
  Education worth sharing, from the creators of the TED talks (ideas worth sharing).

- **JANE GOODALL'S ROOTS & SHOOTS (WWW.ROOTSNSHOOTS.ORG. UK)**
  An education programme for young people to encourage children to implement practical positive change for people, animals and the environment by providing teachers with free resources and activities.

- **30 DAYS WILD (WWW.ACTION.WILDLIFETRUSTS.ORG)**
  An annual nature challenge from The Wildlife Trusts encouraging families to get outside and do one wild thing a day throughout the month of June.

- **THE WORLD WILDLIFE FUND (WWW.WWF.ORG.UK/LEARN)**
  The 'learn' section of the WWF website has 'fascinating facts' about the planet and its wildlife as well as lots of ideas for nature-based crafts and activities.

- **YOUNG CLIMATE WARRIORS (WWW.YOUNGCLIMATEWARRIORS.ORG)**
  Sign up for a free weekly email that contains a challenge for kids to undertake that helps with the climate crisis.

- **CLIMATE PSYCHOLOGY ALLIANCE PODCAST**
  Talking with children about climate change (www.climatepsychologyalliance.org/podcasts/370-3-talking-with-children-about-climate-change)

- **NATIONAL GEOGRAPHIC KIDS - WHAT IS CLIMATE CHANGE? (WWW.NATGEOKIDS.COM/UK/PRIMARY-RESOURCE/CLIMATE-CHANGE-CHALLENGE-PRIMARY-RESOURCE/)**
  A teaching resource to help children think about the impact of human activity on the Earth, and how this can lead to climate change.

- **NASA CLIMATE KIDS (WWW.CLIMATEKIDS.NASA.GOV)**
  Age-appropriate articles, videos and games about climate change from NASA.

The teenage years

The teenage years have a reputation for being difficult – the hormones, the angst, the need to fit in, trying to work out who we are and what we stand for. And I think that in the light of the climate crisis, it's become even more fraught. Our teenagers are making their way in a world where they have not only the usual worries and concerns, but also a very real concern over what their adult lives might look like, and an awareness of the damage that has been done to the planet that they will have to make their lives on.

Research by CBBC's *Newsround* in 2020 questioned over 2000 young people aged 8–16 about their attitudes to climate change and the environment, and found the following:

- 80 per cent said that the problem of climate change was important to them.
- Just 3 per cent said the environment wasn't important to them.
- 73 per cent were worried about the state of the planet, and 22 per cent were very worried.
- Nearly 60 per cent said that they're worried about the impact climate change will have on their lives.
- Nearly two thirds don't believe that people in power are listening to them enough.
- More than 40 per cent don't trust adults to tackle the challenges needed to help mitigate climate change.

These stats break my heart.

Not only are today's youngsters growing up with all the usual teenage stuff going on, as well as the additional challenges presented by growing up in an online world, but many of them are fully aware that the planet they will step out into as adults may not be a safe place; a place where they can live in comfort and security, and bring up their own children.

Eco-anxiety

This is a term which we're increasingly hearing being talked about in the media, especially with reference to young people. Patrick Kennedy-Williams and Megan Kennedy-Woodard run an organisation called Climate Psychologists where they provide psychological support for individuals, communities, families and professionals who are committed to saving the planet. I asked them some questions…

Q What is eco-anxiety? (On that note, is it eco-anxiety, or climate-anxiety, or does it not really matter?)
A Climate-anxiety (or eco-anxiety, it is used interchangeably!) has been described by the American Psychological Association as a 'chronic fear of environmental doom'. The effects can range from person to person. Commonly reported difficulties can obviously include anxiety – including feelings of panic and dread. However, it can be broader than this. People may experience other responses such as grief, anger and powerlessness. These might lead to problems sleeping or eating, or, crucially, making people feel less engaged with finding solutions to tackling climate change or reducing their carbon footprint.

Q Are you seeing it in young people?
A We are relying at the moment on data from questionnaires to answer this question, though they are being published all over the world. They seem to suggest that younger people might be more likely to experience anxiety and other strong emotions as a result of climate change. In the UK for example, one study showed that 34 per cent of the British public experienced anxiety as a result of environmental emergency (29 per cent of whom described feeling overwhelmed).

However, this figure rose to 40 per cent in young people. Generally, rates seem to be higher in young people, though we are still working on answering this question more thoroughly.

Q **Are there any age groups amongst young people where you're seeing it more?**
A Although we're still gathering that data, we were actually surprised to find that primary age children were reporting concerns, having initially assumed it would be more of a concern for secondary school age young people.

Q **As parents, how would we recognise the signs?**
A Age is an important factor to consider. Younger children may exhibit 'magical thinking', which means that they are trying to make sense of information (and misinformation) that they receive. One parent said that their child would scowl at a person smoking a cigarette in the street because they thought it was contributing to global warming. Teenagers may retreat in or express intense feelings of anger and contempt. It's OK to ask kids what they know and how it makes them feel. You can support them to talk about it and when they say what they're feeling, acknowledge its validity and allow space for that feeling to be.

Q **At what point does it go from a very rational and sensible response to the situation, to something that a young person might need some help with?**
A This is a really important question. It's important to say that climate-anxiety has not yet been formally recognised as a mental health disorder, and there are many (both researchers and people who have experienced climate-anxiety) who argue that it shouldn't be. Because climate change is a real existential threat. Research continues to be done to try and answer the question of how climate-anxiety manifests itself, and how best it can be overcome.

Climate-anxiety (or 'eco-anxiety') has become a commonplace term in the media, which is a good thing, in terms of helping people understand their experiences, and to put the issue on the agenda.

However, it's important to stress that in many ways, we are talking about a very normal response to a very real and present threat. So we want to be sure we aren't pathologising (making a disease of something that isn't a disease) people's responses to climate change, or suggesting this is necessarily a serious and debilitating mental health condition for people.

Where it becomes an issue ultimately comes down to the individual – their wellbeing, sleep, etc., and if it impacts on their ability to go about their daily life, or prevents them from being able to engage in solutions to climate change.

Q What can we do as parents if we're concerned that a young person we know is suffering from eco-anxiety?

A Again, active listening, being present and supportive of their emotions. Communication and connection is vital, also having an idea of actions that you can take with them to combat climate change as a family. If you are really concerned, a psychologist may be able to help them manage this worry if it is becoming too much and impacting on their ability to enjoy things, disrupting sleep or becoming more than a worry.

Q What are things that we can do to help (ourselves and others) if we're feeling anxious about the climate crisis?

A In many ways, the cure to climate change is also the cure to climate-anxiety – action. There seems to be a fairly consistent message, from psychologists, researchers and people who have experienced climate-anxiety, that taking action, and engaging in solutions, can result in feeling a sense of agency, which is very good at combatting anxiety and hopelessness and also happens to be good for the planet!

Also, stay connected with people, share your worries. People also report finding mindfulness and relaxation to be beneficial, and getting into nature.

Take practical steps to make an environmental difference – beach clean-ups, or litter picking in your local park. Campaign to local government. Good eco-decisions can be contagious. You may find that you inspire and motivate others with your actions, too.

But crucially, track your progress and celebrate your successes. It's so important to recognise any small steps you take towards lowering your carbon footprint.

Remember that it's better to have a million people trying to help the planet, than one person doing it perfectly. Allow yourself to disengage from the issue now and then. It's a marathon, not a sprint.

Here are Patrick Kennedy-Williams and Megan Kennedy-Woodard's top tips for parents on talking to their children about climate change.

- **Remember that you do not need to be a climate expert** It's OK to explore learning together. If your child asks a question you can't answer immediately, respond by saying: 'What a great question. Let me look into that so I can answer it properly.'
- **Try to validate, rather than minimise, children's emotions** If children express anxiety, it's much better to say: 'It's OK to feel worried. Here is what we can do about it,' than to say: 'Don't worry. It's all fine.' But always try to support this emotion with suggestions for positive action.
- **Negative information hits harder** Bad or threatening facts tend to resonate more strongly – and therefore stick in the mind. So try to balance one piece of negative news with three pieces of positive news. Have some examples of good climate-related news ready – for example, successful conservation projects.
- **For younger children, keep it local and tangible** Suggest litter picks and school events. For teenagers, encourage them to stay connected at a wider level – help them write to their MP, take part in protests and join local communities and campaigns.
- **Set practical goals as a family and follow through** Record and celebrate your climate successes together (even a piece of paper on the fridge door). Reinforce the message that small actions can make a big difference.

Not all teens though will engage in the climate crisis. It might drive us nuts that they'll happily go on a climate strike and yet seem incapable of putting the recycling in the right bins, or turning out the bloody lights. But I think we owe it to them, as a generation, regardless of how engaged individual children are, to support them. To listen, to help them to articulate their anger and their grief that the future they face is so uncertain, through no fault of their own. To lead by example and model the simple changes that can be made at home, even if they don't seem to be taking the slightest notice. And to empower them to know that their voices matter, and that they really can make a difference.

At the same time, I think there's a delicate balance to be struck between empowering them, at the same time as making it clear that this isn't all on them. It's not their issue and theirs alone to fix – that's a hell of a burden for anyone to feel under, let alone a teenager trying to figure out their way in the world. Let them know they aren't alone in worrying about this, that although it might not always seem like it, there are adults moving heaven and earth to create the changes needed.

Our kids aren't quite there yet (9 and 11 at the time of writing), so I can't speak from the experience of bringing up happy, self-assured, confident, empathetic, kind and well-rounded young people who are not only aware of the climate crisis, but who feel empowered to make a difference. And I guess that if you're reading this book, that's kind of the outcome that you'd like too. But I've already said that my kids really aren't that engaged. All that might change. Or it might not. They may maintain their levels of mildly interested apathy, they may embrace climate activism, they may rebel and survive on fast food and fast fashion. I have no idea.

TOP TIPS FROM OTHERS FOR BEING SUSTAINABLE(ISH) *AND* TEEN-FRIENDLY

- 'I was a teenager not so long ago. I'd say the biggest thing is being sympathetic to reluctance to change. Teens go through so many changes in a relatively short space of time that adding in big home changes can take a while to accept, and patience is key.' (Holly)
- 'With teenagers I've found that they have an inbuilt desire to see the rosy side and to do the right thing. They will take information too seriously sometimes and can easily become sanctimonious.

Keep it fun and light-hearted – they can take the world very much on their shoulders at this age.' (Ruth)

- 'For me, teenagers are like toddlers: they are bullshit detectors, and they should be building their own morality systems and beliefs. I want them to leave home knowing what they believe in. By showing them the changes I'm making and articulating them and leaving the door open for them to join me, they are making their own journey – and it's working better than me saying "I'm not buying x because y". They see my imperfect journey, or where I'm experimenting.' (Ann)
- 'One of the main things I would say is that they have to "discover" the cause for themselves, and they are immediately less interested if it's something that has come from their parents.' (Anna)

Q+A WITH JOE BRINDLE - TEEN ACTIVIST AND CAMPAIGNER

Eighteen-year-old Joe Brindle is the campaign co-ordinator at Teach the Future (www.teachthefuture.uk), a youth-led campaign to reorientate the entire education system around the climate emergency and ecological crisis, as well as a volunteer campaigner with the UK Student Climate Network (UKSCN) (www.ukscn.org).

I spoke to him to find out firsthand, to hear how some teenagers are engaging around the climate crisis, and to ask his opinions on how parents can help or hinder their teenagers as they navigate these issues:

Q How concerned are you about the future and the climate crisis?
A I'm very concerned. I think most people my age are. We see that our future lives are under threat and it seems like most of the adult population doesn't share this level of concern.

Q When did you start to become aware of the climate crisis?
A I've always known about climate change on a very basic scientific level, but it was only last year that I started to really understand the

true severity of the crisis after watching a documentary [*I asked him which one it was, but he can't remember*]. It was quite a wake-up moment for me, realising that climate change was causing death and poverty across the world now and that my actions are contributing to this.

Q With the youth climate strikes having such brilliant media coverage, it can be easy to think that all students are really engaged around the climate crisis, but I've heard from parents who have teens who are really apathetic about it. Do you see this, too?

A Sometimes yes. I think often it's not that young people aren't concerned, it's that the reality is so daunting and terrifying that they would rather not think about it. After all, why should the responsibility of change be on young people who have less impact but will certainly feel more effects of climate breakdown than their parents have?

Q As parents, if we have young people who really don't seem that bothered about the climate crisis, should we try to get them to engage? If so, have you got any top tips for how we do that?

A Yes … and no. The climate crisis is scary, it's not healthy for young people to be thinking about it all the time, especially as parents might not know the best ways to talk about such a sensitive topic.

Q As parents, is there anything we should avoid doing?

A Forcing difficult/costly environmentally friendly lifestyle changes on your teenagers probably won't go down too well; it's much better to let your teens explore this themselves (maybe with some prompts from parents). This way they will take ownership of these changes and hopefully continue them into their adult lives.

Q How much has being involved in UKSCN influenced your own personal actions and consumption?

A The more I've learnt about climate change (and acted on it), the more I've tried to change things in my life – from going vegetarian to buying mostly secondhand clothes. Being in a community of like-minded young people has definitely helped show me what I can do.

Q How much peer pressure is there, in your experience, either one way or the other, to take part in climate action?
A A decent bit. I know my friends wouldn't have gone on strikes without some pushing from me.

Q Does your mum still have to nag you to put the recycling in the right bins?
A Occasionally, but very rarely these days!

As our children morph from small people who wear the clothes we buy them, (sometimes) eat the food we prepare and are happy to spend time in our company, to young adults with their own opinions and fashion sense, and who pay far more attention to what their friends think than to us, we're going to have to accept that maybe sometimes they will make different choices to those that we would.

But there are still some easy swaps and changes that can be made, or at least put out there as an option for them to consider.

Periods

I quite clearly remember the school visit from 'The Tampax Lady' in the early years of secondary school, where all the girls were shepherded off for 'the talk' and demonstration of sanitary products. It sounds as though things really haven't come on much in the 30 years since I started secondary school – research by environmental charity City to Sea in 2018 found that most of the discussion tends to focus on a narrow range of products and 'rarely touches on disposal', and that 'education is monopolised by leading brands'.

So why does this matter?

- Ninety per cent of a sanitary pad, and 6 per cent of a tampon is plastic.
- In an average pack of sanitary pads, there is the equivalent of four carrier bags' worth of plastic.

- Over 1.5–2 **billion** are flushed away each year in the UK alone.
- During beach cleans, an average of nine tampon applicators were found for every kilometre of beach in the UK.
- Sanitary products are the fifth most common item found on Europe's beaches; more widespread than single-use coffee cups, cutlery or straws.
- By switching to reusable products, you could save up to 94 per cent of your lifetime spend on disposables.

WHAT ARE THE ALTERNATIVES?

Thankfully there are so many more reusable and plastic-free options available now than ever. Obviously this is a hugely personal choice, and potentially a really difficult time for young people, especially when their periods first start. They will be influenced by a whole range of factors, including what their friends use, how heavy their periods are, what you might use as a parent guiding them through, and lots more.

Remember that, as ever, this doesn't have to be an all or nothing choice. If they're more comfortable trying out reusables at home to start with, or don't feel like they could deal with reusables at school, that's absolutely OK. Maybe look at some of the more eco-friendly disposables for school.

'Options regarding periods definitely need discussing. I use a cup but my daughter started her periods at 11 and although I know teenagers can and do use them (I remember testimonials from 20 years ago from teenage competitive swimmers who said they were much better than soggy tampons!), that felt too young to even suggest it to her. I did buy her disposables initially because I know she is very keen to fit in and I wanted reusables to be her choice when and if she wanted to make the switch. She found the reusable pads very uncomfortable, so we swapped over to period pants, which are comfy.'

Rosii

THERE ARE LOADS OF DIFFERENT ALTERNATIVES FOR A MORE PLASTIC-FREE PERIOD. HERE ARE SOME:

1 Organic pads and tampons

Conventional pads and tampons are made using a lot of plastic and chemicals. If you still want to use a disposable product, either all or some of the time, then look for ones made using organic cotton, that are free from perfumes and chlorine.

Natracare (www.natracare.com) do a range that is available online and in Waitrose stores, as well as independent pharmacies, or you can try a subscription service like TOTM (www.totm.com).

2 Reusable tampon applicators

I always feel like these should have the tagline 'not as grim as it sounds'… And it's not, I promise. DAME (www.wearedame.co) are a British business on a mission to 'turn our bathrooms green', and they're starting with tampons. Not only do they produce organic cotton tampons, they've also pioneered and designed a reusable applicator. It works with any brand and any size of non-applicator tampon, is self-cleaning (via its use of a special medical-grade material and some magic 'sanipolymers' that I confess to not really understanding), and comes with a lifetime guarantee.

3 Period pants

These do what they say on the tin – they're pants, but for your period! They're essentially knickers with an absorbent lining, but don't worry, they don't look like massive bulky nappies. There are lots of different brands and styles available, with different absorbencies for light and heavy flow.

To clean, you simply rinse them in cold water (or paddle about on top of them when you're in the shower), then machine wash at 30°C or 40°C with the rest of your washing (don't use fabric softener) and line dry them (don't tumble dry – it can damage the fabric).

When out and about, or at school, you can get discreet waterproof lined bags to pop your used pants in and simply pop on a fresh pair.

Cheeky Wipes (www.cheekywipes.com) do a period starter kit that contains a pair of period pants, a double wet bag (one side for clean, one side for used), reusable panty liners and that all important bar of chocolate.

4 Reusable pads

These work in the same way as regular disposable pads, only you wash them and reuse them instead of throwing them away. Some brands have poppers on to keep them in place, and you can get a variety of thicknesses for different flows. Again, there's a wide variety of different ones on the market. They're washed and cared for in the same way as period pants (*see* previous page).

Wear 'em out pads (www.wearemout.co.uk) are made in the UK, and do a teen gift box containing four reusable pads, an 'out and about bag', and some lovely goodies to 'give them a reassuring hug'.

5 Menstrual cups

I'm a big fan of menstrual cups, having first tried one after having our eldest and not looked back. Back then they weren't all that easy to track down, but now there are a whole range of different makes and types, with some available in high street shops like Boots and Holland & Barrett.

Just be aware that even for adults used to using tampons, cups can be a bit intimidating, so they might not be the first option to reach for if you're having a discussion with your young person about what's available. But it's definitely worth letting them know that they're there.

There's a great 'quiz' online to help work out what brand and make might suit best at www.putacupinit.com/quiz.

Shaving

As/when/if your teenager decides they want to start shaving, there are some options that result in less plastic being thrown away as blades become blunt.

TRADITIONAL SAFETY RAZORS

These usually have a metal handle and it's just the thin strip of the actual blade that is replaced, rather than a blade encased in plastic. They do take a little bit of getting used to, but honestly aren't as scary as they might look/seem. When your blade is blunt, it can be recycled, although for safety, the advice is to collect them in an old food can, then when it's full, twist the top to seal it, and then recycle.

FFS (FFS.CO.UK)

This is a shaving subscription service for women's razors (can't actually see any reason why they couldn't be used for men too). They look much more like the razors we're now used to, and the blades can be collected up and sent back to them for recycling.

SHAVING FOAM/SOAP/BALM ETC.

There is a wide range of plastic-free options available, from shaving soaps, through to ones in a bowl that you use with a traditional shaving brush – the choice is yours!

Deodorant

Many deodorants are packed with chemicals. Choosing a more natural deodorant is not only better for us, but it's better for the planet too.

Here are three to try:

1 Neal's Yard (www.nealsyardremedies.com) do a roll on and a pump spray, both of which are in glass packaging which can be reused at home, or recycled. The roll-ons offer 24-hour protection.
2 Earth Conscious (www.earthconscious.co.uk) use high-quality natural ingredients for their deodorants that are packaged in either cardboard tubes or recyclable metal tins. They do a range of scents, including a 'strong protection' peppermint and spearmint.
3 Wild (www.wearewild.com) make a case from aluminium and recycled plastic that can be refilled. The refills come packaged in bamboo that can either be recycled with your paper and card kerbside, or in your compost bin.

Make-up

I'm not a big one for make-up (mainly due to a complete lack of confidence in how to apply it) but even I remember excitedly buying a 'heather shimmer' lipstick in Boots, and the obligatory Body Shop white musk body spray…

A quick glance at any cosmetics counter will reveal a **lot** of plastic, most of it unrecyclable, and if you dig a little bit deeper, a whole pile of chemicals and quite probably a side order of animal testing. It's maybe not something we give a huge amount of thought to but most make-up really isn't all that ethical. Here are just a few of the issues to think about:

- **CRUELTY-FREE**

  Testing cosmetics on animals is banned here in the UK, but 80 per cent of the world still permits it. Look for the 'Leaping Bunny' logo on products, which means that the brand itself doesn't test on animals, and neither do the ingredient suppliers.

- **ORGANIC**

  Buying organic is a good way to avoid many of the nasty, artificial ingredients that can be used in cosmetics and make-up.

- **FAIRTRADE**

  By looking for products that contain Fairtrade ingredients it means you can be assured that the growers who are producing ingredients are being paid a fair price.

- **PALM OIL**

  Whilst we're now more familiar with looking out for palm-oil-free, or sustainably sourced palm oil in our food products, it might come as a surprise to learn that palm oil or its derivatives are found in around 70 per cent of our cosmetics. Look out for palm-oil-free products, or ones where the brand is committed to sourcing it sustainably. (Also *see* page 159 for more on palm oil.)

• PACKAGING

Most make-up is packaged in plastic, much of which can be very difficult to recycle. There are now some companies doing refills for make-up, and yet more that package in recyclable packaging (plastic bottles are widely recycled kerbside in the UK).

In September 2020, cosmetics brand Maybelline teamed up with Terracycle (www.terracycle.com) for a 'Makeup Not Make Waste' campaign that should see customers able to drop off any brand of beauty product into recycling bins that will be installed in Tesco, Sainsbury's, Superdrug and Boots stores.

MAKE-UP BRANDS TO CHECK OUT

1 Lush (uk.lush.com)
If you're looking for somewhere on the high street where you can go and try out products, then Lush is your best option according to *Ethical Consumer* website's make-up guide (August 2020). They have a robust anti-animal testing stance and are committed to eradicating all traces of palm oil from their supply chain. They also have a growing range of 'naked packaging' and supply some products in glass instead of plastic.

2 Odylique (www.odylique.co.uk)
Handmade in Suffolk, using organic and Fairtrade ingredients, and never tested on animals, it's easy to see why Odylique scores the highest (16.5/20) in the *Ethical Consumer* guide (August 2020).

3 Zao (www.zaoessenceofnature.co.uk)
A wide range of refillable make-up products, available online. Certified cruelty-free by PETA and committed to working on eliminating palm oil from their supply chain.

DID YOU KNOW?

Soap & Glory (Boots), No 7 (Boots) and Superdrug ranges score 1 and 1.5 respectively out of 20 in the Ethical Consumer guide.

When it comes to removing make-up, try to encourage the use of reusable, washable pads, rather than make-up removing wipes. They can be used with make-up remover and then chucked in the wash. If you're already doing the same, it should just be the 'norm'!

Clothes

Clothes are a huge part of our identity and what we wear can shape how we are seen. I don't remember being hugely interested in clothes as a teenager, being more concerned with 'fitting in' than in expressing my innermost thoughts through them, but as our young people grow up, they will be less and less likely to be happy with the clothes we choose for them, and want to start to buy their own.

With a sometimes limited budget and with shopping often done as a group activity with friends, it can be easy to see the appeal of the likes of Primark and H&M – low cost, easily available, and the latest fashions and trends. However, this low cost comes at a price – which is often at the expense of the people making these goods, and the planet.

- The fashion industry produces 10 per cent of all humanity's carbon emissions (more than international flights and maritime shipping combined).
- Up to 85 per cent of textiles go into landfills each year and the equivalent of one garbage truck full of clothes is burned or dumped in a landfill every second.
- The fashion industry is the second-largest consumer of the world's water supply and is responsible for 20 per cent of all industrial water pollution worldwide.

These are shocking stats. And this is big stuff to process. I think it's quite natural to feel frustrated (as an adult, let alone a teenager) to discover these facts, yet to still want to buy fast fashion and fit in with friends.

As ever, in all of this, remember the 'ish'. If you can splash out on a couple of more expensive new ethically sourced items as birthday presents, and maybe they find a few secondhand pieces online, then supplement this with some fast fashion bought with their friends, that's not all bad…

I have a 15-year-old daughter who IS concerned about things like global warming and the oceans but isn't actively doing anything about it; it's like she does and doesn't get the connection. Favourite shops for clothes are Primark and PrettyLittleThing. Fast fashion. One crop top looks much like another to me, and yet one she will be desperate for and the other will get an "are you kidding me" look.

She has just started using Depop [see page 182], but motivation is to make some money and find some bargains, that it is a way of being more sustainable was a surprise.

I think it's finding the right voices to speak to them. If it comes from me I'm told I "don't understand". Anna

Resources for fast fashion facts and information

- *TRUE COST* MOVIE (WWW.TRUECOSTMOVIE.COM)
  A documentary film that pulls back the curtain on fast fashion, and asks us to consider who really pays the price for our clothing.

- *FASHION'S DIRTY SECRETS*
  This is a 2018 BBC documentary that was presented by Stacey Dooley. At the time of writing, sadly it's not currently available on iPlayer, but you can find clips from it on YouTube which are worth watching.

- FASHION REVOLUTION (WWW.FASHIONREVOLUTION. ORG)
  A campaign that started in the aftermath of the Rana Plaza textile factory collapse in 2013, that now sees an annual Fashion Revolution Week each April. There are loads of free resources on the site, including age appropriate resources for young people in the 'educator' section.

ALTERNATIVES TO FAST FASHION

Some teenagers are more than happy to embrace charity shop and vintage shopping, and relish the opportunity to develop their own sense of style. Others, however, will simply want to fit in, to be wearing the same clothes and brands as their friends, and might fear being picked on or singled out for shopping secondhand.

I think this is an area where we have to tread gently, and we have to respect the choices our kids are making. Even if they've sat with you through *The True Cost*, and understand the damage that fast fashion is doing to people and the planet, it might still feel like a huge step to discuss this with their friends, or to risk sticking their head above the parapet and challenging the status quo in their friendship group. That's OK.

If they still want to buy fast fashion, maybe have a chat about how they can keep the clothes they buy in use for longer? About how it's OK to wear the same clothes on multiple occasions, and even to be seen on Instagram in the same clothes (apparently some teenagers won't post pictures of themselves on social media wearing the same clothes more than once).

Online options

Trawling around charity shops might not be every teenager's idea of a fun way of shopping, but there are an increasing number of online options for sourcing secondhand clothes that have more street-cred (is 'street-cred' even a thing any more?).

- DEPOP (WWW.DEPOP.COM)

  This is a 'fashion marketplace' app. It looks a bit like Instagram with the squares, only instead of beautifully curated flat-lays and peonies, all the pictures are of clothes that are for sale. It can be a great way to find the brands and clothes you want for less, and also to sell any unwanted clothes to make a little bit of cash.

  'I have a 16-year-old girl who is customising vintage clothing and refuses to buy new. Depop is the go-to site for used clothing and footwear for teens.' Natasha

- VINTED (WWW.VINTED.CO.UK)

  Vinted is another app-based pre-loved clothes marketplace. Apparently it has a slightly older target market (I saw one comment online that said 'you're more likely to see your mum on there') but still worth checking out.

- BEYOND RETRO (WWW.BEYONDRETRO.COM)

  With both physical stores and an online shop, Beyond Retro 'scours the fashion runways, global street style, edgy editorial … to determine what's next in fashion' and help them to choose what they pick from 'yesterday's clothes'. You can search by era, by brand, or by item, taking your pick from their top picks of vintage clothing.

Swapping

If your teenager has friends of similar size and taste, they might want to get together for a 'swish' or clothes swapping party. They go through their wardrobes, choosing the clothes that they're maybe a bit bored of, and then get together to swap.

'I think most teenagers do this naturally anyway (I'm constantly asking Maisie "whose top is that" and being told it's her best mate's) – and would recoil in horror at it being referred to as "swishing".'

Charlotte, parent to two teenage girls

DID YOU KNOW?

SWOP IT UP (www.swopitup.org) is an organisation run 'for teens by teens' that works within secondary schools to help 'bring a fun and unique way to tackle climate change and fast fashion'. It's like swishing, but cooler (they're on TikTok, that's all I'm saying). And led by the kids.

Renting

Probably more for one-off occasions like proms or balls, renting is an option for those more expensive items that really might only be worn once.

Prom dresses

I'm showing my age here, but proms were only just beginning to be a thing when I left secondary school, and they were certainly nowhere near the all-out limousine and posh frock occasions that they seem to be now.

If your teenager can't be persuaded to rent a dress, or pick up something gorgeous and vintage, then do have a look to see if there is a local charity or project that it can be donated to afterwards. There are schemes all around the country that take prom dress donations and loan them out for free to prom go-ers who might not otherwise be able to afford an outfit for the occasion. Have a look at Prom Ally (www.promally.co.uk).

Making

We didn't so much as learn to thread a needle when I was at school but textiles is now a GCSE option (and beyond) and more and more people are embracing the sewing machine as a way of showcasing their creativity. Sewing is such a useful skill (I would go as far as to say it's a life skill) and there are lots of sewing courses and classes specifically designed for teenagers. Sewing your own clothes gives you a newfound respect for the people who make our shop-bought clothes, and also means that they're far less likely to be discarded without a thought as the fashions change.

Ethical brands

There does seem to be a pretty hefty hole in the market when it comes to ethical teenage brands. Here are a few that might be worth perusing:

- **KNOW THE ORIGIN (WWW.KNOWTHEORIGIN.COM)**

  Fairtrade and organic ethical fashion for men and women – certainly not high street or fast fashion prices, but if your teenager is looking for some 'key pieces' to base the rest of their wardrobe around then definitely worth checking out.

- **LUCY & YAK (WWW.LUCYANDYAK.COM)**

  The fact that I adore Lucy & Yak's dungarees and other clothes might well be enough to put any self-respecting teenager off, but I hope not!

  Their iconic dungarees are made from organic and sustainable fabrics, at a factory in India – each tailor has their own number which they put on the hem of items and you can look on the website to see who actually made your clothes. They also have a Made in Britain range.

- **MUD JEANS (MUDJEANS.EU)**

  Mud Jeans launched a pioneering leasing system in 2013, whereby you rent the jeans, rather than buy them. You can keep them for as long as you want, with a free repair service, or you can swap them for a new pair after a year. The fibres from the jeans are then recycled to create new jeans, creating a truly circular system.

DID YOU KNOW?

Good on You is a free app that's available on iOS and Android, that rates over 2000 fashion brands as 'We Avoid', 'Not Good Enough', 'It's A Start', 'Good' and 'Great', based on their impact on people, the planet and animals. If the brand you like scores badly, you can use the app to find a similar look from a brand with a better rating, and/or send the poorly performing brand a message urging them to up their game.

How sustainable are the high street brands' 'ethical' ranges?

H&M have their 'conscious collection' – to qualify for a 'green tag' garments must contain at least 50 per cent sustainable materials (e.g. organic cotton/recycled polyester) and reassure us that 'by choosing conscious products you help us to make the fashion industry more sustainable'. And Zara have their 'Join Life' collection and aim to make all their clothes from sustainable fabrics by 2025.

Which is great. And when we see massive brands like this start to make noises about sustainable fashion, it tells us that the groundswell of public opinion is starting to shift and that they are hearing demands from their customer base for more ethical products.

HOWEVER. What we really need to address when it comes to fast fashion, is the fast part of it. It is simply not possible to make fast fashion sustainable due to the sheer volume of garments that are produced. Despite being made from more sustainable materials, H&M's conscious collection is still very cheap, and those savings have to be made somewhere. It's still a low quality, high volume system, predicated on encouraging us, the consumers, to buy, buy, buy.

If your teenager still wants to shop on the high street (and as I said, we have to accept that they're not always going to make the same choices that we are) then choosing the conscious collection is still better than picking from the regular range, as it's sending a message to retailers that we want more sustainability in fashion.

HAULTERNATIVES

I'm not sure if 'haul videos' are as popular as they once were, but I'm told they're still a thing. Basically they're a video of someone unpacking their 'haul' of shopping – usually fast fashion, but could be make-up, trainers, etc. They share what they've bought, how much it cost, how excited they are. And these are shared on social media.

They might possibly be dismissed as just a bit of fun, but they're far more damaging than that. They glamorise overconsumption and fast fashion. They normalise these excessive levels of shopping and can make young people watching them feel like this is what they should be doing too.

In an attempt to counter this, Fashion Revolution came up with the idea of a 'haulternative'. In their campaign in 2020 they had eight different haulternatives to choose from, all encouraging us to see our clothes in a different light. From 'broken and beautiful' (sharing visible mends of clothes), to 'clothes swap' (swapping clothes with friends, either online or in real life), to 'love story' (sharing a story about a piece of clothing that means a lot to you) and renting, it's a fabulous way of encouraging us to look at our clothes and how we buy them in a different way.

Devices

We know that constant use of devices is not especially good for either our own mental health or that of our kids, but it's also not especially good for the planet either.

- Around 85 per cent of the carbon footprint of a smartphone comes from its manufacture (the rest is electricity usage for charging etc.).
- There are as many as 60 elements in a smartphone, the mining of which contributes to a whole host of environmental issues and human rights abuses in the places where they are mined.
- Some estimates claim that smartphone lifespans could potentially be 5–10 years, however most of us use them for an average of 12–24 months before upgrading.
- Over 60 per cent of smartphone sales are replacements for existing phones, 90 per cent of which are still perfectly functional.
- Only around 20 per cent of old phones are recycled.

- Emails, text messages and social media usage all need data servers to function, which use up vast amounts of energy keeping them functioning and cool.
- Currently, information and communications technology, as a whole, accounts for more than 2 per cent of global greenhouse gas emissions (for context, aviation is around 2–4 per cent). Scarily, it's predicted that this could be up to 20 per cent of the global total by 2030 based on current trends.

HERE ARE SOME EASY WAYS TO REDUCE YOUR FAMILY'S PHONE FOOTPRINT:

1 Keep your phones in use for as long as possible. According to The Restart Project, a social enterprise encouraging and empowering people to use their electronics longer, if we used every mobile phone sold over a year for just a third longer, it would prevent carbon emissions equal to that of Ireland's annual emissions.

2 Buy a refurbished phone. We did this recently via Envirofone (www.envirofone.com/en-gb).

3 Sell or pass on your old mobile to prolong its useful life.

4 If your phone is broken or too old to get software updates, then ensure it is recycled.

5 Have a look at Fairphone (www.fairphone.com) – smartphones that are designed and produced with minimal environmental impact.

Confession: I looked at Fairphone when my old iPhone stopped accepting software upgrades, and really wanted to love them and buy one. However, the reviews I found were really variable, and I opted instead to go down the secondhand route and buy a refurbished iPhone.

TOP TIPS ON HOW TO RECYCLE YOUR MOBILE PHONE

Up to 80 per cent of a mobile phone is recyclable – don't leave it languishing in a drawer or send it to landfill!

- Most charities will have a mobile phone recycling scheme where they make some money passing on donated phones to mobile phone recycling companies.
- If you buy a new phone from a high street store, ask them how you can recycle your old one – most will provide you with an envelope to send it off for recycling.
- Women's shelters, homeless shelters and refugee charities will often accept donations of mobile phones, so it's worth asking locally to see if there is anywhere that could make use of yours.
- If all else fails, make sure you put your old phone in the 'small electricals' bin at your local recycling centre.

School

In essence, much of the advice for primary school kids (in the previous chapter) with regards to uniforms, shoes and school bags applies here, just on a larger scale.

I'm not sure how many secondary schools have secondhand uniform systems, but that's not to say you won't be able to pick up blazers and branded school stuff pre-loved. It might just be that you have to put feelers out amongst fellow parents, or you might see uniform offered on places like local Facebook buy, sell, swap groups.

When it comes to ethical options for new uniform, the resources for buying ethical options of school basics on page 133 all have sizes that go up to 15–16 years of age, so if you aren't restricted in where you can buy your uniform from, you do have some choices.

Packed lunches may or may not be a feature of your pre-school morning with teenagers, and again, the same principles apply for reducing plastic food packaging, only you will need much larger lunch boxes! There may also be some additional peer pressure and a desire to not be 'the weird one with the beeswax wraps'. If that's the case, have a chat about what would feel like a more comfortable solution for your teenager. Reusing a bread bag can work really well, and might not be quite so obvious as a 'green' solution for friends to comment on.

As kids get older they are more and more likely to want to make their way to school under their own steam. This is a great ready-made eco solution! Most secondary schools have pretty good public transport links, and lots of kids will choose to walk or bike with their friends without any need for nudging from their parents.

From what I've been told by parents with older kids, parental involvement in school life can tail off pretty sharply as soon as they start secondary school. This means that any influence you may have been able to exert as a PTA member or such-like may no longer be there. To influence school policy around eco matters, you may have to make the decision to 'uplevel' and become a governor (not something I think most of us would choose to do lightly!). And in all honesty, this might be the stage where you have to let go a little, and allow your teenager to take on these issues themselves if it's something they feel passionately about.

Many secondary schools are signed up to the Eco-Schools pathway (www.eco-schools.org.uk/secondary-pathway) and actively encourage their young people to take ownership of the eco changes they want the school to embrace – the pathway is designed with pupils in mind and gives them 'every opportunity to show that they really do care about their environmental future'.

Finding their voice

Part of being a teenager, or growing up, is all about finding your voice. Discovering who you are, and what you stand for. Working out what you're prepared to take a stand on. And how you can you make your voice heard.

Teenagers can get very fixated on certain issues (for me it was animal testing), and start to develop a very clear sense of right and wrong. In that development of their values set, there is sometimes very little space for ambiguity – things are either 'good' or 'bad'. And when channelled right that passion, that refusal to be fobbed off, can be a hugely powerful thing.

It's a really important part of growing up, but the thing that I think we as parents, who might have the climate crisis as one of our own drivers, have to beware of is that we have to let our young people find their own voices. They have to find out for themselves the causes that they are passionate about. If they align with ours, that's amazing. If they don't, don't despair. They are feeling their way, testing the water, exploring. And they have the capacity (as we all do) to change their minds, as they grow and as they discover new sources of information, meet new friends, widen their experiences.

Let them explore their thing – if they have one – whether that's animal rights, or veganism, or plastic pollution, or something else entirely unconnected with the environment. The important thing is that they are listened to, and that we help them to feel like their voice matters, and that they can make a difference around the issues they care about.

One of the problems that I think can lead to eco-anxiety (*see* page 166) is the feeling that there is nothing they can do about the issues they care about. I know many young people feel frustrated that the adults in charge aren't taking the action needed to safeguard their futures.

Listen to them. And encourage them to take actions that not only help them to feel like their voices are being heard, but that also help to actually make their voices heard as well.

1 Sign

Online petitions can get a bad rap, and can easily be dismissed as 'clicktivism' (signing a campaign whilst making no other efforts to change your own life) but they DO work!

Ella Daish is a campaigner who is working to eliminate plastic in all menstrual products and she set up a petition on Change.org calling on the major manufacturers to #EndPeriodPlastic (www. change.org/p/make-all-menstrual-products-plastic-free). With over 200,000 signatures on the petition at the time of writing, she has been able to engage in conversations with decision makers at the likes of Tesco, Boots, Li-lets and Bodyform. It has resulted in Sainsbury's, Aldi and Superdrug stopping production of their own plastic tampon applicators (saving over 1.7 tonnes of plastic every year!), and has seen an increase in the number of eco-friendly and reusable options available in many supermarkets and retailers. So these things do work!

2 Write

Write to your MP (you can find out who your MP is at www. theyworkforyou.co.uk). Even if you're under 18, and not yet eligible to vote, that doesn't mean that you don't have a voice and that politicians won't pay attention. Within one election cycle you could easily be a voter, and MPs are increasingly paying more and more attention to the voices of our young people, especially given how much momentum they have gained from the school climate strikes.

Write to brands and retailers – ask them what their policies are. Point out the ones that you disagree with. Ask them what action they're taking on the climate crisis.

3 Vote

When you're old enough to vote, make sure you do! And vote for the party whose policies most closely reflect your own.

You can also vote with your money – who you choose to give your hard-earned money to is a way of voting for the kind of world that you want. It can be hard when you're a young person who maybe doesn't have that much money, but don't forget that NOT spending your money can send a strong message too. So, refusing that upgrade that Apple keep 'reminding' you about, learning to repair your clothes, turning your back on fast fashion – these are all ways of quietly disrupting the status quo, but just because they're quiet doesn't mean they aren't effective.

School strikes

At the time of writing (June 2020) the climate strikes that we became so familiar with in 2019 are on hold as the world locks down due to the coronavirus pandemic. I have no doubt though that they will restart when it's safe to do so, and they have been instrumental in pushing the climate crisis not only up the political agenda, but also up our own personal agendas too.

They have been an outlet for some of the anger and the grief that many young people are feeling, and personally I have been so heartened to see so many people empowered to make their voices heard around what is a truly pivotal issue for their generations and those to come.

Many adults have joined in with the climate strikes, especially supporting younger school children who want to attend. But there are other ways that you can show your support for the school strikers. The UK Student Climate Network (UKSCN) has a page on their website (www.ukscn.org) – a guide for our adult allies – and has kindly allowed me to share the key points here:

1 **Enable your child, or a child you care for, to attend Youth Strike 4 Climate demonstrations**
There are template permission letters if you need them on the website, and also some advice to discuss with your child how to stay safe at a strike.

2 **Encourage schools and local authorities to be supportive of children striking for climate justice**
Use any links you might have to those in authority in schools and local authorities to explain why you're supporting the demonstrations. If you are in a position of power, declare your support for students.

3 **Let your local media know that you support the climate strikes**
Again, there are template letters to help you to do this on the website.

4 **Let young people lead**
It is important the Youth Strike 4 Climate movement is led by young people and that it is their voices that we hear.

5 **Take action yourself**
Talk to other adults in your workplace and family about why you're supporting the strikes. Share your thoughts on social media, and also use your social media profiles to give a platform to young people's voices. Additionally, you can donate money to support students in taking further climate action.

Books for teens

- *HOW TO BREAK UP WITH FAST FASHION: A GUILT-FREE GUIDE TO CHANGING THE WAY YOU SHOP – FOR GOOD*; LAUREN BRAVO, HEADLINE HOME, 2020

   If you've ever wanted a guidebook to walk you through how to dress with less impact and more style, this is the book for you!

- *NO-ONE IS TOO SMALL TO MAKE A DIFFERENCE*; GRETA THUNBERG, PENGUIN, 2019

   This is a small book, but it packs a big punch. A collection of some of Greta's most powerful speeches, all in one place. Impossible to read and not feel compelled to act.

- *THIS IS NOT A DRILL: AN EXTINCTION REBELLION HANDBOOK*; EXTINCTION REBELLION; PENGUIN, 2019

   I have to confess to not having read this book, but for anyone wanting to 'up the anti' and get more informed about, and more involved in, environmental protest, it looks to be a pretty comprehensive guide.

- *WHO CARES WINS: REASONS FOR OPTIMISM IN OUR CHANGING WORLD*; LILY COLE, PENGUIN LIFE, 2020

   'If you dare to care it's a head f*ck' has to be my favourite line from this book. It's really well-researched and Lily Cole, model and eco-entrepreneur, has been able to interview many of the world's leading voices to put together this truthful, yet optimistic, book.

- *THE FUTURE WE CHOOSE: SURVIVING THE CLIMATE CRISIS*; CHRISTIANA FIGUERES AND TOM RIVETT-CARNAC, MANILLA PRESS, 2020

   Christiana Figueres and Tom Rivett-Carnac were fundamental in uniting the world in the historic 2015 Paris Climate Agreement. Their book begins by outlining the two very different futures we could be facing: one terrifying, and the other much more inviting. They then set out the choices we need to make.

- *THERE IS NO PLANET B: A HANDBOOK FOR THE MAKE OR BREAK YEARS*; MIKE BERNERS-LEE, CAMBRIDGE UNIVERSITY PRESS, 2019

    This does what it says on the tin and really is a handbook for the make or break year – a hugely comprehensive guide covering questions like 'Should we frack?' and 'Should I buy an electric car?' through to 'Does it all come down to population?' and 'How can I work out who and what to trust?' It also contains a great appendix of climate change basics and a useful glossary of climate terms.

Films for teens

NB Depending on the age and sensitivities of your teen, it might be worth watching these on your own first, before deciding whether they are something that might be helpful in starting a discussion.

- *2040* (WWW.WHATSYOUR2040.COM)
    - 'An aspirational journey to discover what the future could look like if we simply embraced the best that exists today.'

- *THE STORY OF STUFF* (WWW.STORYOFSTUFF.ORG)
    - A short animated documentary by Annie Leonard about the lifecycle of material goods. There's also loads of other short films on the website, like *The Story of Bottled Water*, and *The Story of Mircofibers*, alongside the team's first feature length film, *The Story of Plastics*, released in April 2020.

- *BEFORE THE FLOOD* (WWW.BEFORETHEFLOOD.COM)
    - A 2016 documentary about climate change, featuring Leonardo DiCaprio. It's quite hard-hitting, but does give some hope at the end.

- *CHASING ICE* (WWW.CHASINGICE.COM)
    - A 2012 documentary following environmental photographer James Balog as he deploys time-lapse cameras to capture a multiyear record of the world's changing glaciers.

- ANYTHING BY DAVID ATTENBOROUGH
    - Especially *Our Planet*; *Blue Planet II*; *Seven Worlds, One Planet*; *Climate Change – Extinction: the Facts*.

5 QUICK WINS WITH TEENS (ARE THERE ANY QUICK WINS WITH TEENS?)

1 **Start a gentle conversation about the climate crisis** Maybe watch a film or documentary together, and discuss how it makes them feel afterwards.

2 **#Idontbuyit (www.globalactionplan.org.uk/com-passion-not-consumerism/i-dont-buy-it)** Ask your teen to scroll through their own Instagram feed for 60 seconds and make a note of how many ads and sponsored posts they see. This is a suggestion from Global Action Plan as part of their #Idontbuyit campaign to raise awareness around just how insidious advertising is and the steps that we can take to consume more thoughtfully. There're loads of resources on the website for parents as to how to engage with their teens around consumption.

3 **Let them take the lead** It might be that their 'thing' is being vegan, or plastic-free, or going on climate strikes. It's unlikely to be turning the lights off, or not standing staring in front of an open fridge door. Try not to nag too much about the little stuff, and let them come to things in their own time.

4 **Model sustainable(ish) behaviours** If it feels completely normal to eat regular meat-free meals, to shop secondhand, to carry reusables, then these are all hopefully habits that your teen will either carry on with, or at least won't feel totally alien to them.

5 **Listen** Accept that your priorities might not be their priorities right now. Listen to what they have to say, and keep those all-important channels of communication open.

Over to you

What will you try? Ideally sit down with your teens and ask them if there's anything they want to try. Brainstorm three to four things you could have a go at as a family and list them below:

Action	Timeframe
1.	
2.	
3.	
4.	

Resources

- **UK STUDENT CLIMATE NETWORK (WWW.UKSCN.ORG)**
  Information and resources about UK Youth Strike 4 Climate events, alongside how to strike safely, and information for parents wanting to support their child's climate action.

- **GLOBAL ACTION PLAN (WWW.GLOBALACTIONPLAN.ORG.UK)**
  As well as their #Idontbuyit campaign (*see* page 196), Global Action Plan have a youth panel of 18–25-year-olds who feel passionate about addressing climate change.

- **WORLD WILDLIFE FUND (WWF)**
  The WWF website has a whole host of resources including a page on climate change resources for youth groups (https://www.wwf.org.uk/get-involved/youth-groups/resources/climate-change-activities) and a badge scheme for Green Ambassadors.

- **ECO-SCHOOLS (WWW.ECO-SCHOOLS.ORG.UK)**

  As well as the resources for primary schools discussed in Chapter 6 there are also resources for secondary schools looking to be more eco-friendly, and importantly, engage their students around climate action.

- **UNICEF'S VOICES OF YOUTH (WWW.VOICESOFYOUTH.ORG)**

  A dedicated platform for young advocates to offer inspiring and original insights on issues that matter to them. There's a section specifically on climate change.

- **KIDS CLIMATE ACTION NETWORK (WWW.KIDSCLIMATEACTION.ORG)**

  Although based in Oxford, there are resources on here that can be applied across the UK (and beyond).

- **KIDS AGAINST PLASTIC (WWW.KIDSAGAINSTPLASTIC.CO.UK)**

  A charity set up by UK teenagers Amy and Ella Meek that aims to raise awareness and understanding of the problems caused by plastic misuse; encourage and support others to become 'plastic clever' and reduce single-use plastics; and empower children and young people to believe they can make a difference.

Conclusion

I'm never quite sure how to end books. How to neatly summarise everything that's been discussed and tie it up with a neat bow and a motivational quote.

The climate crisis is a HUGE issue. It's complex, it's overwhelming, it's scary as hell. It will come as no surprise to hear that there is no neat bow, but I do have a couple of motivational quotes! It can be easy to feel hopeless and as if the die is already cast.

It's not. We still have time to turn this around. To quote Sir David Attenborough:

'What we do in the next 20 years will determine the future for all life on earth.'

So no pressure then.

But the point is that we still have a choice. In 20 years' time, when a child born today will be all grown-up, there will be no going back. The decisions that will affect their adult life are being made by each and every one of us today. There is still time. There is still hope. But to quote another environmental icon, this time Greta Thunberg:

'Instead of looking for hope, look for action. Then, and only then, will hope come.'

We don't have time anymore to simply hope that governments will step up and take action. To hope that businesses will do the right thing. We have to take action ourselves. Action that helps to lower our own impact, and action that puts pressure on governments and businesses to step up too.

That action can be imperfect action (and will be the majority of the time). That doesn't mean it's not making a difference. It might feel like a drop in the ocean, but to coin a particularly cheesy motivational quote, all of those drops add up to make the ocean.

Pick one thing. Make one change. That one change gives you the momentum and the motivation that make the next change easier. And the next one, and the next one. When you're exhausted, overwhelmed and scared, know that you're not alone. That it's OK to pause awhile and get your breath back. And then pick yourself up and focus on putting one foot in front of the other. No change is too small.

Keep talking. To your partner if you have one – this can feel like a heavy responsibility to bear on your own. To your friends, and your wider family. To your MP, to brands and retailers – make your own voice heard as you encourage your kids to do the same. Talk to your kids. Model the changes and behaviours that you want your child to emulate. Talk about the choices you're making and why. You don't need to be constantly ramming it down their throats, but being open about your reasons for doing what you're doing is powerful stuff.

Greta calls on us to 'act as if you loved your children above all else'. And we don't need to *act*: we do love our children above all else.

Now we need to make sure that our actions are giving them the future they deserve.

Acknowledgements

My thanks again to the brilliant team at Green Tree and Bloomsbury for being so lovely to work with, and so enthusiastic about a second book! Special thanks to Charlotte Croft and Holly Jarrald for polishing my ideas and ramblings into a much more cohesive format!

Thanks as well to my lovely agent Kate who was on maternity leave for much of the period during which this book was coming to life (congratulations Kate and family!) and to Rachel for stepping in to cover so seamlessly.

I'm not sure many books written during 2020 will fail to acknowledge the tireless work of our amazing key workers and NHS staff who have kept the country running during these unprecedented times – thank you all for your hard work and the sacrifices you've so selflessly made.

Which brings me on to thank my husband, a key worker himself, who instead of getting a bit of downtime at the weekends had to pick up the reins of entertaining the kids whilst I attempted to hide myself away (usually unsuccessfully, it has to be said…) and write.

And of course, thanks to our kids, William and Samuel, for being so bloody resilient during lockdown, for putting up with some of Mummy's more crazy eco-ideas, and for both learning to make a cracking cup of tea.

Lastly, I said it in *The Sustainable(ish) Living Guide*, but I make no apologies for saying it again here – a massive thank you to YOU. For being curious, for reading, getting informed, and for making a difference.

References

Introduction

- Carbon footprint of having a child: *How bad are bananas?: The carbon footprint of everything*, Mike Berners-Lee, Green Profile, 2020, p157
- 2018 IPCC report: https://www.ipcc.ch/2018/10/08/summary-for-policymakers-of-ipcc-special-report-on-global-warming-of-1-5c-approved-by-governments/ (accessed 13th June 2020)
- Currently on course for 3–5 °C temperature rise: https://uk.reuters.com/article/us-climate-change-un/global-temperatures-on-track-for-3-5-degree-rise-by-2100-u-n-idUKKCN1NY186 (accessed 13th June 2020)
- We are already seeing climate refugees: https://www.unhcr.org/uk/climate-change-and-disasters.html (accessed 13th June 2020)
- We see thousands of ads a day: https://web.archive.org/web/20200320191358/https:/www.nytimes.com/2007/01/15/business/media/15everywhere.html (accessed 13th June 2020)

Chapter 1: Some basic principles

- More than 60 per cent of global greenhouse gas emissions are a result of household consumption: https://onlinelibrary.wiley.com/doi/abs/10.1111/jiec.12371 (accessed 13th June 2020)
- We're running out of landfill space: https://app.croneri.co.uk/whats-new/uk-running-out-landfill-space (accessed 13th June 2020)
- BBCs *The Secret Life of Landfill*: https://www.bbc.co.uk/programmes/b0bgpc2f (accessed 13th June 2020)
- Mattresses for babies: https://www.lullabytrust.org.uk/safer-sleep-advice/mattresses-and-bedding/ (accessed 13th June 2020)
- Secondhand car seats: https://www.childcarseats.org.uk/choosing-using/second-hand-child-seats/ (accessed 13th June 2020)

- Secondhand bike helmets: https://www.rospa.com/Home-Safety/Advice/Product/Second-hand-Goods/ (accessed 13th June 2020)
- Only 10–30 per cent of the clothes received by charity shops are actually sold on in the UK: *Clothing poverty: the hidden world of fast fashion and secondhand clothes*, Andrew Brooks, Zed Books, 2015
- China places ban on plastic recycling imports: https://www.nationalgeographic.com/magazine/2019/06/china-plastic-waste-ban-impacting-countries-worldwide/ (accessed 13th June 2020)
- A land mass the size of Canada and India put together is used to grow food that is never eaten: http://www.fao.org/fileadmin/templates/nr/sustainability_pathways/docs/Factsheet_FOOD-WASTAGE.pdf (accessed 13th June 2020)
- If food waste were a country, it would be the third largest emitter: http://www.fao.org/3/i3347e/i3347e.pdf (accessed 13th June 2020)
- Fifty per cent of food waste occurs in the home: https://wrap.org.uk/sites/files/wrap/Food_%20surplus_and_waste_in_the_UK_key_facts_Jan_2020.pdf (accessed 13th June 2020)
- Increase in bag for life use: https://www.bbc.co.uk/news/uk-50579077 (accessed 13th June 2020)
- Water bottles: https://refill.org.uk/about/why-refill/ (accessed 13th June 2020)
- Collectively in the UK we use 7.5million disposable coffee cups a day: https://www.bristolwastecompany.co.uk/forcupssake/ (accessed 13th June 2020)
- Americans use enough straws each day to circle the planet 2.5 times: https://namepa.net/2018/07/13/2018-7-13-plastic-straws-an-environmental-problem-gaining-importance-to-the-public-and-the-marine-industry/ (accessed 13th June 2020)
- Mums hold the purse strings: https://www.mintel.com/press-centre/social-and-lifestyle/mums-both-queen-and-king-of-the-household-as-she-leads-purchasing-decisions-across-all-categories (accessed 13th June 2020)

Chapter 2: Pre-baby

- Births in the UK: https://www.ons.gov.uk/peoplepopulationandcommunity/birthsdeathsandmarriages/livebirths (accessed 13th June 2020)
- Finnish babies sleep in cardboard boxes: https://www.bbc.co.uk/news/magazine-22751415 (accessed 13th June 2020)

Chapter 3: New baby

- 3 billion nappies are thrown away each year in the UK: https://www.wrap.org.uk/content/real-nappies-overview (accessed 13th June 2020)
- Disposable nappies account for 2–3 per cent of all household waste: https://www.wrap.org.uk/content/real-nappies-overview (accessed 13th June 2020)

- By the time they're potty trained the average baby will have used 4000–6000 disposable nappies, or 20–30 reusable ones: https://www.wrap.org.uk/content/real-nappies-overview (accessed 13th June 2020)
- Reusable nappies can save parents between £200–500 over the course of a child's nappy wearing time, and even more if they're used for subsequent children: https://www.wrap.org.uk/content/real-nappies-overview (accessed 13th June 2020)
- By using real nappies, the average household waste of families with babies can be halved! https://www.wrap.org.uk/content/real-nappies-overview (accessed 13th June 2020)
- Around 25 per cent of a disposable nappy is plastic: https://www.thenappylady.co.uk/news/plastic-disposable-single-use-v-cloth-nappies.html (accessed 13th June 2020)
- Impact of laundry choices on carbon footprint of reusable nappies: An updated lifecycle assessment study for disposable and reusable nappies – Science Report – SC010018/SR2 (accessed 13th June 2020)
- 10.8 billion wipes are used each year. https://www.citytosea.org.uk/campaign/be-a-good-ahole/ (accessed 13th June 2020)
- Four hundred per cent increase in wet wipes found on beaches: https://www.mcsuk.org/press/call-for-better-labelling-on-flushables (accessed 13th June 2020)
- Nestlé: https://www.ethicalconsumer.org/company-profile/nestle-sa (accessed 13th June 2020)
- Babies generally outgrow seven clothing sizes in their first two years: https://www.nct.org.uk/get-involved/corporate-partnerships/bundlee (accessed 13th June 2020)
- One third of parents have thrown away perfectly wearable outgrown baby clothes because they didn't know what else to do with them: https://www.bigpicturecollective.com/blog-2/2019/9/30/the-little-loop (accessed 13th June 2020)

Chapter 4: Bigger babies

- Little Freddie's recycling scheme: http://www.enval.com/little-freddie-enval-recycling-initiative/ (accessed 13th June 2020)
- Bamboo cups can release toxic chemicals when used for hot drinks: https://www.chemistryworld.com/news/reusable-bamboo-mugs-leach-dangerous-amounts-of-formaldehyde-and-melamine/4010950.article (accessed 13th June 2020)

Chapter 5: Toddlers and pre-schoolers

- Average spend on toys: https://www.npdgroup.co.uk/wps/portal/npd/uk/news/press-releases/collectables-see-off-brexit-blues-as-the-toy-market-rises-by-more-than-6/ (accessed 13th June 2020)

- Kids' magazines: https://www.toynews-online.biz/2018/06/19/uk-kids-magazines-plastic-toy-tat-purge-is-top-of-the-agenda-says-egmont/ (accessed 13th June 2020)
- Ella and Caitlin McEwan: https://www.bbc.co.uk/news/uk-england-hampshire-49069522 (accessed 13th June 2020)
- Ofsted and eco-schools: https://www.eco-schools.org.uk/about/benefits-of-joining/ (accessed 13th June 2020)
- Eco glitter study by Anglia Ruskin University – Glitter Litter could be damaging rivers: https://aru.ac.uk/news/glitter-litter-could-be-damaging-rivers-study (accessed 20th October 2020)

Chapter 6: Primary school age kids

- School run pollution: https://www.bbc.co.uk/news/av/uk-england-south-yorkshire-49960950/how-do-you-breathe-less-pollution-on-school-run (accessed 13th June 2020)
- Aviation currently makes up around 2–4 per cent of global greenhouse gas emissions: https://www.theguardian.com/business/2019/sep/19/airlines-co2-emissions-rising-up-to-70-faster-than-predicted (accessed 13th June 2020)
- Only around 5 per cent of the world's population actually use aeroplanes: https://www.dw.com/en/to-fly-or-not-to-fly-the-environmental-cost-of-air-travel/a-42090155 (accessed 13th June 2020)
- The US, China and the EU account for 55 per cent of all aviation based emissions: https://www.theguardian.com/business/2019/sep/19/airlines-co2-emissions-rising-up-to-70-faster-than-predicted (accessed 13th June 2020)
- Brits fly more than any nation – twice as much as Americans: http://afreeride.org/about/ (accessed 13th June 2020)
- On an individual level, there is no other human activity that emits as much over such a short period of time as aviation: https://www.dw.com/en/to-fly-or-not-to-fly-the-environmental-cost-of-air-travel/a-42090155 (accessed 13th June 2020)
- 270,000 hectares of precious rainforest are cleared annually for palm oil growth: https://www.rainforest-rescue.org/topics/palm-oil (accessed 13th June 2020)
- Every hour 300 football fields of precious remaining forest is being ploughed to the ground across South East Asia: https://www.orangutan.org.au/about-orangutans/palm-oil/ (accessed 13th June 2020)

Chapter 7: The teenage years

- CBBC's *Newsround* climate-anxiety study: https://www.bbc.co.uk/newsround/51451737 (accessed 13th June 2020)
- Period education: https://www.citytosea.org.uk/campaign/plastic-free-periods/rethink-periods/why-we-are-doing-this/ (accessed 13th June 2020)

- Sanitary items on beaches: https://ec.europa.eu/environment/circular-economy/pdf/single-use_plastics_impact_assessment.pdf (accessed 13th June 2020)
- Fast fashion stats: https://www.weforum.org/agenda/2020/01/fashion-industry-carbon-unsustainable-environment-pollution/ (accessed 13th June 2020)
- Around 85 per cent of the carbon footprint of a smartphone comes from its manufacture: https://www.compareandrecycle.co.uk/blog/environmental-impact-of-your-smartphone (accessed 13th June 2020)
- Smartphone lifespans: https://en.reset.org/knowledge/ecological-impact-mobile-phones (accessed 13th June 2020)
- Over 60 per cent of smartphone sales are replacements for existing phones, 90 per cent of which are still perfectly functional: https://en.reset.org/knowledge/ecological-impact-mobile-phones (accessed 13th June 2020)
- Global greenhouse gas emissions from data centres: https://www.nature.com/articles/d41586-018-06610-y (accessed 13th June 2020)

Index